Typical of the Times

Typical of the Times:
Growing Up in the Culture of Spectacle

Jaime Clarke

Roundabout Press   2022

Published by
Roundabout Press
PO Box 370310
West Hartford, CT 06137

ISBN: 9781948072083
Library of Congress Cataloguing-in-Publication Data is available on file

FIRST PRINTING September 2022
10   9   8   7   6   5   4   3   2   1

For Mary and Max

Acknowledgments

My thanks to

Hayden Bennett
Josephine Bergin
Pete Hausler
Dan Pope

Typical of the Times

Our memory is made up of our individual memories and our collective memories. The two are intimately linked.

—*1Q84*, by Haruki Murakami

THAT VANESSA WILLIAMS THING WAS RIGHT AROUND THE time of the mcdonald's massacre you couldn't turn on a television without hearing about those poor innocents just eating lunch and then a circumstance occurs like earlier when the teenage sears security guard shooed away the kids gathered around the in-store video game console and the youngest boy whose father would become the host of america's most wanted ended up dead at the hands of a child predator or the time before that when someone was putting something in tylenol and that's the prevailing fear in the backseat of the gray family ford ltd except maybe the troublingly named indian school road the map of phoenix a geometric marvel you don't think you've ever seen a city made of a grid but over the years it will become apparent that unlike other places you've lived everything about phoenix was master-planned except the freeway to los angeles which ends in a pile of concrete and slumbering construction vehicles a block from the house on the west side your father and younger brother rented in advance you and your youngest brother and mother staying behind in rapid city for reasons you may never know like all the childhood questions that just remain questions like why did everyone mail away for those free gum balls made out of a new kind of sugar and you suspect the answers are unsatisfying as answers anyway and so you don't bother two bryan adams concerts in one summer is the result yes you dreamed at the first concert in

rapid city of meeting a girl and had no idea that months later at your
second time through the set list that you'd be holding hands with a
girl who would ultimately get you kicked out of phoenix veterans
memorial coliseum but you think the move to the empty upper deck
is for something more than hand-holding and not for smoking
cigarettes which security would spot pretty quickly yes you had
broken up with your first phoenix girlfriend on her birthday while
lying in the dark on the phone unaware that your chronic
nosebleeding wasn't tears on your cheek all those afternoons going
over to the first girlfriend's trailer across from your new school how
many new schools you didn't care to remember the first girlfriend's
mother was always home and let you hold hands on the couch while
watching television but you weren't allowed down the hall except to
use the bathroom and only when the first girlfriend was firmly
stationed in the front room or sometimes the kitchen the first
girlfriend's friend who lived in the trailer park had one of those
arms that wasn't all the way an arm more than the def leppard
drummer after he crashed his corvette into a brick wall but still not
like everyone else and you didn't care if people stared but she did yes
you broke up with the first girlfriend for the reasons time immemorial
that men break up with women but you didn't yet understand that
until you did   that one afternoon when the girl-who-would-
ultimately-get-you-kicked-out-of-the-bryan-adams-concert's sister
stalked into the bathroom and poured cold water on you both in the
shower parents that both work is a thing you have in common
including an overwhelming interest in sexual exploration her lost
fake fingernail found in your boxers at the rest stop on her family's
trip to california you imagined you were daniel and she agreed she
could be ali from the karate kid when you snapped pictures at the
same golf n' stuff as in the movie her grandmother made you sleep
on her couch in indio and the curios and doilies were unnerving and
you asked to bunk in with her older brother much later the
grandmother's house is confused in your mind with that of the actor
ray milland when you learn he died in indio madonna sings her new

song like a virgin at the video music awards wearing a wedding dress and a bustier vh1 debuted a couple of hours after the def leppard drummer crashed his corvette come to think of it the time the girl was inconsolable when her five-year-old stepbrother was killed run over in the street is the prevailing memory of that time also the eighth-grade graduation trip to disneyland purchased by selling tom-wat door-to-door because a lot of kids will never graduate high school the teacups and the hotel with piss-stained elevators and strawberry hill and california coolers after curfew because the basketball coach is on watch california coolers with the basketball coach that one time he drove the starting five from the basketball team to magic mountain you sandwiched between the center cradling a barrel of unwrapped smarties double lollies and the team's point guard nursing the wine cooler so his allergy to alcohol didn't flare or the time with the limo driven by the basketball coach his side job for the actual graduation stumbling out of the limo for more wine coolers spotted by someone who knew the girl's mother the girl's mother telling your mother in the checkout line at the alpha beta but the time the girlfriend was inconsolable is the prevailing memory that was when everything was new and burnished for memory keeping moving to phoenix the day before classes start a new kid yet again after being new again and again and again memories in boxes the kids in south dakota didn't seem to know anything about what happened to john lennon that made all the teachers at your school in north dakota hang their heads or all those hostages they let go or when another someone tried to impress that actress months later or when kiss came on without makeup or fractured fairy tales or the bloodhound gang and vice versa the kids in williston were left void of knowledge of the girl from somewhere in the east being invited to russia after she wrote a letter to yuri andropov which made you start writing letters to celebrities to see if they'd write back though they mostly sent signed pictures of themselves or the handful of videos on the new music channel or michael jackson's thriller video or what happened to michael making that pepsi commercial or the first woman on the supreme court or when that famous actress fell off the boat and died or the first test tube baby it all happened after none of it connected in your mind at least important to remember all the new names easier to make friends if you seemed like you were always there call out someone's name make them feel known so that you can be too first calling attention to yourself in some way that wasn't too obvious was always the next step not like ozzy and the dove or lawn chair larry in montana it was reading the most books and winning lunch with your teacher the batman skit the previous year performed with the assent of your second-grade teacher the jar of ash from mount saint helens you swept from your driveway the nude poster you claimed to have of the actress who played daisy on the dukes of hazzard in north dakota it was lighting fires with the neighbor kids learning hey jude on the piano as a favor to your neighbor who was mad like your teachers about the john lennon thing the variety show like the mandrells' you proposed to emcee in the gym to impress the girl who tantalized you by giving you a pocket radio and telling you to listen to dr demento at the same moment she was lying in bed listening in south dakota it was fingerprinting the teacher's assistant you were in love with making your parents drive you to the local bottling company for enough carbonated water to make strawberry soda as a science experiment for your class racking up the high score on pac-man and dig dug and centipede and donkey kong at the arcade showing the older kids how to seesaw a comb across your hand to quickly toggle the buttons for defender marathon sessions of space invaders and breakout on the atari at home waiting for your parents to come home from work writing the hardy boys–inspired novel you bragged about writing to your teacher who called you on it and who agreed to type it up and send it to publishers who all rejected it which burned more when that kid published his star wars quiz book the music teacher knew you were lying when you said you went to a country music convention at the civic center and that you'd gotten up on stage and sang a conway twitty song made you sing a song in front of the class to see if you could sing dating the seventh grader at the junior high your sixth-grade teacher passing notes to her one neighbor to another you and your younger brother each play a song on the piano on television your piano teacher arranging it your name glowing from the television as you play silver bells it seems like magic learning the moonwalk to go with the beaded glove you and your friend billy fashioned for the purpose of walking around rushmore mall getting stares writing and directing your own version of the tv show whiz kids with the av equipment from the junior high after seeing wargames a hundred times and the milwaukee 414s on the cover of newsweek also because the world stopped for the final episode of m*a*s*h you still can't think of it without welling up when you think of hawkeye's inability to say good-bye he only had to say it once change is sometimes change but sometimes it isn't in phoenix the first order of business is getting out of the gifted and talented program really just a place to hide away the restless and hyperactive kids the bus would come for you in north dakota in the middle of the school day to transport you to the high school where the gifted program was high school kids throwing snowballs hard at you at recess the new kid new again but just on thursdays locking the gifted classroom door on the way out with the teacher's purse and keys inside does the trick in phoenix as does the unrevealed fact that the eighth grade in phoenix is a repeat of the seventh grade in rapid city which means coasting academically speaking everyone thinking you're some kind of genius but you only care about being freed to reinvent yourself shedding all the computer nonsense in favor of sports and music a pantomime of the guitar solo in let's go crazy you standing on a chair the yardstick quivering in your hand like prince's ax wins unanimous approval from all who witness it and naturally you form an air band with some newly made friends from the basketball team for which you're a starting guard by virtue of being tall the air band you call phantasm after the horror movie you watched with the team on a friday night at the basketball coach's house sworn to secrecy about the booze the

basketball coach a former phoenix police officer but something
funny about the story never really know for sure but don't care as
long as he keeps offering discounts on limos from his family limo
company it always seems cool when the basketball coach shows up
as the limo driver means he'll buy for you too like the night everyone
had their wits scared away from watching phantasm which rumor
had it was directed by a teenager and then you want to make a
movie too but after the band which wins the school talent show
handily you lip-synching the words to open arms and don't stop so
convincingly that you incur a fan club among sixth-grade girls who
start turning out for the home basketball games and then again in
the bleachers during softball season phantasm is asked to headline
the next parent-teacher dinner and the keyboardist drummer and
lead guitarist agree with your suggestion of performing a couple of
bryan adams songs run to you and heaven make the cut the whole
band shops for stage clothes at the millers outpost at westridge mall
keeping the receipts and tucking the tags in so everything can be
returned the following day there are perks to celebrity you come to
know when you follow some girls into the bathroom as a joke and
even though you get hauled into the principal's office nothing
happens you sell the box of lunch tickets the printer dropped and no
one wants to believe it's really you doing it you toilet-paper the gym
teacher's car and he knows it's you and your friends but nothing
happens you break curfew at the hotel in anaheim on the graduation
trip to disneyland and again nothing happens not just the basketball
coach watching your back but other teachers too except for your
homeroom teacher who notices and you can tell she's unamused at
all the free passes but then you rise through the ranks of spellers and
represent your school at the state competition lasting a few rounds
before going out on the word yawl which you spell with an o instead
of an a but even that defeat is treated like a victory and back at
school there are congratulations aplenty someone jokingly asks if
you're on the recording for we are the world and you laugh but
there's also menace in the joke and you think careful careful careful

you don't really understand backlash until that spring when new coke debuts and even though the soda delivers everything it promises there's such a stink about it that they bring back the old coke and there's a rumor that the guy who came up with the idea was fired and you think about that maybe more than you should when you're selected as the valedictorian speaker and over the summer as you think ahead to your freshman year the summer of repeated viewings of back to the future and miami vice reruns if only to stay out of the crushing heat waiting for the sun to set to walk the neighborhood with your boom box playing van halen's 1984 crashing party lines for however many cents a minute at night the summer all the girls dressed like madonna consternation that the like a virgin tour wasn't coming to phoenix the rumor that madonna had a revolving bed onstage while she was singing or maybe it was prince another tour that wasn't coming to phoenix though it didn't matter because you had to be seventeen to go everyone wondering why wild sexual rumors as guesses the kid who had a copy of purple rain on betamax the kid who asked where's the beef so much people started avoiding him that was the summer of live aid the kids starving in ethiopia phil collins playing the london show and then flying to america on the concorde for the other show the same day jack nicholson everywhere that day too everyone cooing over a band called u2 taking the job at the fish and chips down the street from your future high school slinging monsterburgers dixie dogs fish sandwiches fries with everything using the money to catch weird science your new favorite movie replacing st elmo's fire your other favorite movie but tied with the breakfast club and better off dead then the rock hudson jokes but no jokes about ryan white the kid born the same year as you whom they wouldn't let go to school because he had aids from a blood transfusion parents of other kids and teachers scared out of their minds john cougar and michael jackson and elton john and kareem abdul-jabbar became his friends alyssa milano gave him a kiss ryan white proved you could get aids if you weren't a homosexual which some people seemed to fear more than aids but he was just a little boy another innocent in a circumstance like the girl who wrote the letter and went to russia then died in a small plane crash somewhere back east right before you start high school and you think how can someone get all the way to russia and back only to die in a small plane crash in america it doesn't make any sense but it recalls the not-too-distant past in rapid city when your entire sixth-grade class wrote letters to lyle alzado the l.a. raiders football player your teacher knew from when she tutored him in college no answer to the letters which didn't upset you except you thought maybe your teacher one of your favorites was embarrassed that someone she once knew and helped had turned his back on her now that he was famous like madonna had to her own flesh and blood the year of madonna really desperately seeking susan marrying sean penn sean penn firing at swarming paparazzi in helicopters waiting in the parking lot of a 7-eleven to ambush someone safe but sympathetic who could buy you the penthouse magazine with madonna on the cover the photos not as good as the ones you'd seen in rapid city on rodeo weekend the dumpsters full of magazines you'd never heard of a hierarchy quickly developed oui penthouse playboy penetration the difference maker in your mind but not just yours madonna is the first celebrity you've seen fully nude and even after you've hightailed it out of the 7-eleven parking lot you can't believe what you're seeing like the time someone on the basketball team had a vhs copy of faces of death or the film you needed a permission slip to see in junior high the choose your own adventure about how babies are born everyone says michael jackson now owns all the songs written by the beatles which is confusing the question about whether or not your grade-school popularity will transfer with you to high school is answered pretty quickly as you become an anonymous freshman face in the small mexican town on the outskirts of phoenix the high school mostly mexican too but white kids bused in from everywhere until the mexicans are a minority again those mexicans you get to know through your after-school job at the fish and chips some of them even recognizing you from over

the summer especially those you began to favor with free food
including the security guard a local you've cultivated the saxophone
that has lain dormant since the seventh grade reawakens in your
first-period band class marching season that fall playing halftime at
home and away games riding the bus hassled at work for needing
friday nights off the busiest of the week don't you know but band is
your entrée into the world of upperclassmen who take a liking to
you like others in south dakota and north dakota and montana did
previously and you don't try to analyze it just say yes to hanging out
with them at their houses late into the night drinking their parents'
alcohol or to the midnight showing of the rocky horror picture show
some of the upperclassmen are in the drama club too throwing toast
and rice at the screen after your shift at the fish and chips has ended
then driving around until all hours of the night looking for alleged
parties sometimes in other school districts someone knows someone
who is having a party or not breaking into the resorts ringing
camelback mountain to use the pool if all else fails that fall you
adopt wholeheartedly the fashions of sonny crockett which gets you
noticed in good and bad ways but mostly good when it comes to
girls and the blonde whose locker is on your row and who doesn't
wear a bra finally gives in to your badgering her for a date when you
ask her to the ac/dc concert your colleague at the fish and chips who
spent the summer drawing in pencil the scene of the seven dwarfs
all puffing from the same bong offers to drive for a ticket to the
concert he'll even throw in a bottle of southern comfort but he hits
on the blonde all night annoying the hell out of you but it doesn't
really matter because she's gone by the encore falling in with some
older friends she knows from you don't want to know where but you
have better luck with the junior who is the section leader of the
flutes your first high school girlfriend and she takes some guff for
dating a freshman but any who know you are okay with it same for
whoever nominates you for homecoming prince you feel like it's a
lock everyone saying it's going to be you but then it's not and not
even really close a local kid whose friends apparently all voted for

him wins and you file that lesson away all music must come with warning labels now if the lyrics are graphic you watch huddled around the television in the classroom as the challenger explodes upon liftoff there's an atomic meltdown at chernobyl a place you don't really know where that is campaign season and your friends suggest you run for sophomore class president make your mark for jaime clarke on your signs and out of your mouth and when the lopsided victory is yours there's yet another lesson about which is coveted more the beauty contest for homecoming prince or the academic honor of being class president the difference between duckie and blane even on the makeshift stage at thomas mall before it is demolished strutting with the other teenage models booked through the dubious agency you joined with your friend the surfer who orders his clothes from the international male catalog the agency books you for a commercial for an italian restaurant says bring your saxophone you never know if the commercial runs never paid for anything the only money exchanging hands is yours for head shots dressing up in various costumes against various backdrops your vanity from the time the girl in the water park in south dakota thought you were corey hart and other instances like that and maybe even the lost homecoming prince election driving you to believe but you tell no one and your surfer friend is equally mum there's a lot of talk about who is going to be participating in hands across america the guy from st elsewhere coming to phoenix to be part of the chain the idea something ferris bueller might come up with like yours to take the senior girl you meet playing in the orchestra pit of the high school production of the hobbit on a one-day trip to disneyland limo to and from the airport courtesy of your old friend the basketball coach airline ticket courtesy of your fish and chips fortune you can't believe when she says yes but then the day is overwhelmed with the gesture the spontaneity second-guessed with questions about if you do things like this all the time and you say no even though you know you do and when you're not you spend too much time daydreaming grand schemes that you desire with all your heart to

come true you always the star of the show another self-aggrandizer
like that fake jimmy swaggart who gets wal-mart to pull rolling
stone magazine from its shelves or all those celebrities in the
antidrug stop the madness video including old friend and
noncorrespondent lyle alzado the world is full of attention seekers it
seems sean penn punching a musician at a club in los angeles eg or
anyone on entertainment tonight or a current affair which becomes
obsessed with the preppy murderer in new york only because he's
handsome but new york city is as far away as the moon from the hot
and humid summer you spend working and scheming about your
sophomore year at a loss when not actually in school an environment
you thrive in the endless possibilities not true of the summer or
school vacations which are all just work boredom work sophomore
year starts off with the inxs concert at the mesa amphitheatre the
pastel-colored crowd sweating in the summer that won't end and
when it's over some of the crowd follows the limo you and your
friends rented to ferry you to and from the party thinking maybe
you're the band but your friend sticks his head out of the window
and the jig is up and the cars fall back everyone laughing but some
annoyed not to have teased the ruse further to at least see if any girls
were in the trailing cars no one can answer the question about
whether or not max headroom is a real person or not the freshman
sax player in your section agreeing to become your girlfriend which
is mostly ceremonial since she's a mormon and can't date until she's
sixteen and even then only in groups of other mormons is the word
but it hardly matters your relationship mostly revolves around band
practice and traveling to away games and band competitions you
going to her parents' house after school but before your shift at the
fish and chips to shoot pool and listen to music or watch movies
while her mother lurks somewhere her mormon friends like you and
vice versa the good crowd from school the kids all the teachers like
even the security guard who catches you and your girlfriend and
some other friends off campus during school hours your idea all the
way not realizing residents in the small town would look out their

windows and call campus security but them not realizing you have campus security in your back pocket feeding them and their families for free at the fish and chips your girlfriend panicking her reputation surely taking the biggest hit but the security guard recognizes you and gives everyone a ride to the edge of the football field as the bell for the next class rings he'll say he couldn't find anyone and you'll continue to repay the favor for as long as you work at the fish and chips wishing you had the same influence over the security guard at a rival high school when he finds you hiding in the men's room while your friend and fellow student council officer searches the campus for her boyfriend to confront him about cheating the security guard seems pleased to drag you to the principal's office the principal yelling about calling the police charging you with trespassing and as your friend arrives in the clutches of a second security guard you remember that a girl from a party you found yourself at over the summer is on the student council at the rival high school and you claim to be her cousin from south dakota the security guard not buying it but the principal seeing a way out of the mess that threatens to turn an otherwise ordinary day into a vortex of procedure and you pretend to cower under a tongue-lashing the security guard escorting you both to the parking lot a tale that becomes as legendary as the flames shooting from your saxophone at halftime of the homecoming game your section leader rigging camping stoves in his and yours passing a lighter at a key moment on the field everyone astonished even the band teacher who is both angry and awed by the pyrotechnics you didn't consider that he could get in trouble with the school but you and your section leader disappear the camping stoves and no one asks you about it you try for another piece of legend when in your official capacity as assistant to one of the chemistry teachers during your free period you leak some test answers not knowing that there are two sets of answers so when the girls you're trying to impress answer their test with the exact sequence of answers for the test they're not taking you get busted and your free period is converted to detention for the rest of

the semester said detention held in the band room and run by the
band teacher who lets you practice or leave early the papers full of
oliver north and his secretary fawn hall and iran-contra the term
plausible deniability floating through conversations a term you like
there's a rumor rob lowe is dating the secretary and also a rumor
about richard gere the heavy metal group judas priest is ordered to
stand trial over two teens in nevada who shot each other on a
playground one of them dying instantly the other maimed and
living a few more years their parents think they did it because of
subliminal messages in judas priest's music the mormon car salesman
elected governor without a majority cancels martin luther king jr
day calling it an illegal holiday also calling black children
pickaninnies and telling black people they don't need a holiday they
need jobs oh and the time he told a jewish delegation that america
was a christian nation and boy did those japanese businessmen's
eyes get round when they found out how many golf courses arizona
had and the retribution is sure but slow playing out for months and
years to come the kid in your class who disappears for long stretches
of time is liberace's protégé and the proximity of celebrity at your
tiny high school in a tiny town on the outskirts of phoenix is
unbelievable there's a rumor his hands are insured for millions no
one really seems to know him one kid calls him a fag like liberace
and the protégé punches the kid with his million-dollar fists the
protégé presents an interesting shot at political redemption after the
disastrous first semester of your reign as sophomore class president
not outwardly disastrous but a failure in your eyes the homecoming
float the largest piece of legislation on each class's agenda your idea
to get a corporate sponsor met with confusion and more confusion
when said corporate sponsor is the local mcdonald's so that the
sophomore class offering is a floating advertisement for mcdonald's
during construction in the jv quarterback's backyard everyone
working diligently to re-create the golden arches out of chicken
wire and crepe paper you're amazed both at how bad the idea is and
how readily everyone was willing to undertake it the spring class

fund-raiser is a chance to erase those memories and after approaching the protégé with the idea you present the protégé in concert as your class fund-raiser some officers had no idea about the protégé and some don't know who liberace is but once again everyone just goes along and so the concert is booked the lone apple macintosh that constitutes the school's computer lab is used to create the promotional flyer ads are taken out in the local papers the protégé has a piano delivered to the school auditorium he's contractually obligated to use only a certain brand of piano and the night of the concert you pace with the protégé backstage as the auditorium fills to half its capacity the protégé says i can fill radio city music hall but not a high school auditorium and you give a nervous laugh but he's not really kidding much later you'll think about this over and over and over but then you go on with the show by parting the stage curtains and introducing the protégé whose playing mesmerizes the audience the success of the fund-raiser inspires you to fill a notebook with the names of bands you intend to contact via letter about playing at your high school raising even more money ac dc yes u2 of course quiet riot and duran duran and depeche mode and then a list of bands possibly looking for a way to expand their audience but the absence of congratulations on arranging the concert with liberace's protégé is disappointing it's like the concert never happened except for those in the audience no students really by the way just adults who enjoyed liberace's music and absent the accolades the whole thing feels hollow unappreciation leads to some bitterness and the sudden realization that your friends will be graduating leaving you among your fellow sophomores most of them not your friends most of them resentful of your friendship with upperclassmen or indifferent but regardless there's no way to come back into the fold and your one other friend from grade school the one who went to private school appears as a lifeline and the private-school friend arranges a shadow day where you follow him around campus and attend class with him the private school is an all-boys catholic school which is full of non-catholics since it's one of the only private schools in phoenix and is generally regarded as the best the words college prep in its name the giveaway the private school sits on central avenue the dividing point between east phoenix where the haves live and west phoenix where the have-nots like you live the school is populated mostly with the haves which suits you just fine though in your heart you know you'll never really be friends with any of them and that your friends will be have-nots like your private-school friend but that's okay because you really just want the association not to have to pretend that you're a have though you and your private-school friend angle to get a pair of fake rolexes from mexico and hoover up all the polo shirts at the used-clothing store after your application is accepted for the fall why you failed to mention either your shadow day or your application to your girlfriend balloons as a glaring cruelty when she learns about it from someone else the confrontation one of the terrible moments of your life up to that point you have no answer fumbling with an excuse that you didn't think you'd be accepted though you never doubted that for a minute looking good on paper will become an obsession your girlfriend is never fully assuaged even though you promise you never thought of it as a betrayal and you craft a good joke about dating a mormon girl while attending a catholic school which gets you both past it also you remind her about your newly minted driver's license which means no more hitching rides to her house after school meaning you can visit more often which you promise to do and mean it at the time you utter it not realizing the true freedom a license and the used ford mustang ii your parents give you bestow the preacher on the sunday-morning tv show loses his job because he drugged and raped his secretary along with another preacher which completely validates and supports everything you think about religion same again when the other preacher gets caught with a prostitute months later and same again but this time about politics when the photo of the senator running for president and the model on his lap is everywhere everything is just a cloak for attracting people's attention sometimes sexual attending the baptist church with your private-school friend a megachurch down the street from the private school mostly to use the phenomenal exercise and sports facilities in an effort to curb the toll nightly meals at the fish and chips are taking on your body surprised to see the rocker alice cooper in the front pew with his family his daughter's baptism on the agenda of the program in your lap you really don't have any idea who alice cooper is but know he's someone famous who lives in phoenix but he just looks like a father and a husband in church after watching your friends graduate and leave high school behind forever you move a little farther west into a neighborhood being terrorized by a rapist the starlight rapist is the name named for the neighborhood but it sounds like an album and no one goes out after dark only men are walking dogs suddenly you and your private-school friend go for jogs because you highly doubt that anything will happen to you and you both openly hope to catch the pervert roaming the streets talking tough about the violence you're capable of everyone listening to the new u2 album the first few bars of the first song everywhere like weather someone initiates a recall of the mormon car salesman governor and then the news becomes just about that the story advancing incrementally sometimes without any new facts just everyone's anger and embarrassment especially when the governor digs in and doubles down like politicians always seem to just like the senator with the girl on his lap did when everyone said he was finished they're always the last to know you trade the ford mustang ii in on a midnight blue volkswagen rabbit a wolfsburg edition which just means the color and seat covers are different but feels important for the start of your new school akin to owning a nagel painting your parents are upset because the mustang ii was almost paid off but you can't go to a fancy prep school in a mustang ii you and your private-school friend get vanity plates too yours is my hare and his is beemer for obvious reasons your junior year starts and it's like moving again nothing that happened before really happened or is relevant and everything is in the now saying the private school's name perks every listener's ears and for maybe the first time in your life you feel the benefit of exclusivity membership in a club you want to belong to but know you probably don't and never will your grades were good enough to get in but only because the public school was easy and probably only really because your teachers wrote stellar recommendations but the private school is hard harder than you anticipated and then because you live on the west side of phoenix and not the east you don't really enjoy the social aspect of your new peer group certainly not the company of the girls who attend the all-girls private school adjacent to yours no one has heard of the area where you live and because you didn't go to any of the same middle or junior schools as the other students and because your family doesn't know any of the other families you're marked as an outsider from day one and you take note of the fact knowing it'll come into play for the rest of your life but rather than be daunted by it you just let it go you aren't even sure what it is you hoped to gain by becoming friends with rich kids you don't need a loan for chrissakes and they have no idea how or why they're rich they just enjoy the designation even the son of one of the phoenix 40 a list of the rich and powerful in town who offers to sell you some cocaine at lunch somewhere in texas a baby falls through the tiny opening of an abandoned well and for two days the television documents the rescue the baby miraculously okay when she's pulled free your english teacher the one who kisses the ass of the kid whose father is a famous golfer and the other kid whose father is a state politician and has a terribly lame joke about meeting his wife she was a stockbroker and he was looking to invest and the joke is he went in looking for stocks and came out with a bond assigns the great gatsby and you devour it thinking it's a book about you astonished by the similarities between your story and jay gatsby's and you become convinced that your girlfriend is daisy at least narratively and you adopt the attitude that your love for each other is doomed especially as you seem to be spending less and less time together owing to your commute downtown and then your racing back west to work your paycheck suddenly suffering the heavy tax of keeping up appearances at the private school but also because you frankly spend time cruising the

east side of phoenix a part of town previously unknown to you
exploring the roads lined with expensive homes even wending to
the top of camelback mountain where the priciest homes of all are
perched and also the biltmore area with its boutique shops and
exclusive restaurants and the difference between this world and
yours solidifies all of it bifurcated by the private school that resides
geographically between the two and maybe not just geographically
just like the two eggs in gatsby though you start to think less of jay
gatsby and more about f scott fitzgerald famous and rich and then
broke and forgotten in the same lifetime but immortal in death and
that seems more desirable than money something to really strive for
but the how is too hard to parse and you drop it until you're watching
the credits roll on the midnight showing of less than zero and see
that the movie which you consider powerful for its examination of
the importance of loyal friendships is based on a novel and later you
do a little sniffing around the phoenix public library and learn that
the author is more like fitzgerald than not and maybe that's the
blueprint you read the author's second book which isn't as well
received as the first just like fitzgerald and it's about the doings of
kids at a college in the woods of vermont and you truthfully can't
make much of it but the striking difference between the author
photos of the first two books is something to note the party scenes
in the book exceed anything you experience hanging out with your
graduated high school friends in their new digs in tempe the college
town built up around arizona state university one friend living in a
dorm with beer bottle caps pressed into the ceiling of the hall so
many they gleam like a metallic rainbow and the other moving into
a newly built pink stucco apartment complex across the street from
campus for students only miles better than the other apartment
complexes which are really just old cinder-block motels repainted
and repainted all with crumbling swimming pools ringed with
coeds catching rays it's quickly clear that all the cool kids will be
living at the new complex the rental application asks for fraternity
affiliation so rival frat members aren't accidentally booked into the

same four-person apartment the complex deciding who will live with whom the only drawback but no one seems to mind for access to the sand volleyball court and the sparkling pool but really for the weekend parties so legendary that kids at your new private school have heard of them the apartments are identically furnished so that while the locations of the parties are different each weekend the parties have the feel of having picked up where the other ones left off all of the faces nameless to you and to everyone you think but no one cares you first hear about the u2 concerts at sun devil stadium at one of these parties and the notion that the tickets are only five dollars seems like drunken rambling but radio stations all over town start broadcasting that the band will play two shows on consecutive days to film a documentary and to ensure the stadium is full both nights all tickets are only five dollars word is celebrities from hollywood are driving through the desert in their limos to attend and you and your private-school friend score some tickets excited at the prospect even if the seats are terrible all the way up toward the top of the bowl some kids have tickets for both nights which you find slightly annoying but you also wish you could go both times but when you're actually at the show you're distracted by the murder of the owner of the fish and chips two nights prior someone knocking on his door while he was sitting down to dinner in his apartment the owner always lived frugally even though his chain of fish and chips was successful and mostly all-cash operations and while the apartment where he lived was in a better part of town he was still shot point blank through the chest when he opened the door his dinner still cooling on the table and in the days after leading up to christmas it becomes known that the killer was after the sack of silver coins commemorating the fish and chips' fortieth anniversary the owner kept in his closet the local pawn shops are put on alert and just like in the movies the killer tries to pawn the coins and is arrested and revealed to be the investigator hired by the insurance company the fish and chips owner had applied to for better rates the recall election of the car salesman governor is set and your private-

school classmate's dad who is a congressman agrees to run though
before the election can happen the car salesman governor is indicted
for this and that and removed as governor you actually like the
classmate he was the kid who sat in front of you on your shadow day
way back when and he actually spoke to you unlike the others and
you identified him as an all-right guy right off though you never
really became friends with him or the kid running for student
government who gave his campaign speech in the gymnasium and
listed one of his hobbies as being an avid beaver hunter and everyone
shrieked ending the kid's candidacy and earning him a week's
suspension but also a bit of legend which far outweighed the
punishment though not so for the senior who appeared on camera
during a news investigation about boondockers in the desert kids
gathering with illegally purloined alcohol and then scattering drunk
and whatever else behind the wheels of their cars the senior agreeing
to be interviewed on camera and telling the reporter that nothing
could stop them from partying which although it was probably true
did abruptly end his studies at the private school when he was
expelled as not representative of the school's student body you have
more pressing concerns though as you realize your relationship with
your high school girlfriend has completely crumbled you never see
each other there aren't enough hours but also maybe you're just a
little more interested in your reincarnation as a private-school
student the part-time job at the law firm down the street from the
private school another piece of the new puzzle the idea of quitting
the filthy fish and chips job the ultimate goal but for now you must
work both especially since you traded in the new volkswagen you've
hardly made any payments on for a red nissan pulsar nx with t-tops
and a vanity plate that reads o2b yng taking on an outrageous
monthly car payment but appearances are becoming more important
every day exhausting as it can be the two lives being lived
simultaneously and so you initiate the breakup with your high
school girlfriend in a cowardly way by writing a letter and asking
her to meet you a month later to give everyone time to think about

everything and when the month is over you're kind of surprised that she shows up at the time and place you suggested but the surprise quickly turns to chagrin when you realize she's rightly been simmering for a month and pulls out her own letter and reads it to you cataloging all your sins and drops it at your feet you knowing you deserve every word but the devastation is sudden and uncontrollable and you can barely remember driving the freeway back home your old friend who looks like anthony michael hall attempting to flag you down from his front yard as you turn onto your street but you don't want him to see you that way not knowing it's your last chance to talk with him never knowing what he wanted to say to you that day or why he shot himself months later his parents quietly moving back to colorado you are excused from classes to attend a seminar on teen suicide held at the convention center and your friend thinks it's a great ruse for getting out of class and tags along so the experience becomes a goof and not the chance to heal or at least to be a little less bewildered your private-school friend has a friend who lives in rancho palos verdes outside of los angeles and you both bomb through the desert to the cool foggy shores of the rich suburb your friend's friend is a nationally ranked motocross racer who tours the country on his sponsor's dime which is in your mind pretty legendary except you don't care anything about motocross but traveling here and there to perform before adoring crowds as a teenager engenders some jealousy but the motocross racer is a cool guy and he takes you and your private-school friend to a couple of parties sneaks you into the local yacht club though you get caught and escorted out the ocean air filling your desert-dried lungs hey there's a nude beach nearby the motocross friend says and you park above overlooking the beach but it's the opposite of what you hoped for just families frolicking in the surf without any clothes a bummer for sure but you're perked up by the motocross racer's saying that lyle alzado lives in his neighborhood and as you pass in front of the palatial white estate behind a tall iron gate the distance between where you are and where you've been feels oceanic and it makes you a little sad to think of your sixth-grade self penning the unanswered fan letter and you think maybe it would be funny to ring the doorbell and bring it up with alzado who has retired from football to become an actor but who will really become famous a few years later when he dies from a brain tumor he claims was brought on by his steroid use but you don't that fall your history teacher wants everyone to volunteer for a political campaign during the current election cycle the incumbent democratic candidate for senator's office across the street from campus the obvious choice but just to be contrary you answer an ad for the republican challenger someone you've never heard of a financial planner of some kind who hasn't a prayer of winning and when you report to the financial planner's house in the gated biltmore estates you learn the campaign team is just you and the financial planner's son who has dropped out of the university of arizona and put his band's music on hold to work on his father's campaign the mission that day is to put up campaign billboards but the posthole digger is impotent against the hard desert floor and you don't get one sign up the incumbent wins by a couple of hundred thousand votes and you feel no way about it not like you did in the mock vote for president in the fourth grade when you were sure carter would win and woke up to the complete opposite the credit for working on the financial planner's campaign can't offset the reality of your college algebra teacher holding you after to tell you that you are failing and might not graduate in the spring you beg for another chance and he says there are two jaime clarkes which one will show up and you promise the right one even though he never does and you're ultimately busted down to a lower-level math class that you almost don't pass though you get an a in your christian service class which has you volunteering at the children's crisis nursery where kids are taken when the police remove them from their homes for whatever reason the popular volunteer spot is the state mental institution the stories of all the loonies acted out back on campus to slack jaws and disbelief and mocking laughter but you know you won't last a day there and so the children's crisis nursery it is just playing with kids during your shift and they're just kids and love having fun and it's sad only when you remember the high chain-link fence around the building and the orders not to let any parents who might be wailing outside in to see their kids the investigator for the insurance company who murdered the owner of the fish and chips goes on trial and the schedule is arranged so that you and your private-school friend can attend along with some other employees the murderer looks like someone's grandfather the windowless courtroom antiseptic and overly acoustic and simply boring there's no doubt the guy did it the procedure is just to string together the narrative in a cohesive way so that everyone can put the matter behind them before christmas the year punctuated by news that one of the popular wrestlers back at your old public school has asked your ex-girlfriend out to the christmas formal and blind with jealousy you undertake a successful campaign to win her back which is a win you needed everyone needs a win it seems not just your new private-school friend who is living in his own apartment off the freeway hiding from his deranged father but also the woman and her young daughter living in the economy housing next door to the new fish and chips location you transfer to when you and your private-school friend have a falling out over your going back with your high school girlfriend the private-school friend annoyed to lose you as part of a recent foursome with two vietnamese girls you've been spending quality time with you just as a wingman but you put the kibosh on the whole thing which sends your private-school friend to the moon and you don't speak ever again necessitating the transfer to the new location where you get your new private-school friend a job the new private-school friend's deranged father learns he's working there and shows up waving a gun on the sidewalk you roll the metal window guards down and cower by the fry cookers waiting for the police who come and your new private-school friend watches while his father is placed in the back of a squad car the woman and her young daughter ask you about it later they weren't home when it happened and you shrug even though you were for a

moment fearful and change the subject and ask them if they have
their christmas tree yet and the mother says it's either the tree or
something to put under it which guts you and you play santa and
buy a big tree with lots of ornaments and tinsel and surprise the
woman and her daughter who seem embarrassed and then you are
too when the tree won't fit easily into the tiny apartment the
awkwardness increased when the little girl shows off the christmas
tree hanging on the wall made from toilet paper tubes and cotton
balls the last time you see either of them because they quit coming
around a serial killer everyone describes as handsome is executed in
florida you and your high school girlfriend easily fall back into the
old routine of never seeing each other especially as you start spending
more and more of your free time with your old public-school friends
out in tempe hatching a plan to move in with them in the summer
after your high school graduation a plan you're up front about with
your high school girlfriend but it's theoretical and besides she's never
been to your house or met your parents so what does it really matter
the relationship is kept within the confines of the school you no
longer attend and her front room which you frequent less and less
and church dances different from the rave you attend at an old
warehouse in downtown phoenix with adults you don't know your
college friend procuring the address the streets dark and crime-
ridden so you slip out to move your car under a streetlight and when
you return you see a large black man dancing naked and when your
eyes adjust you see others are naked too and your friend grabs you
and says it's time to go the actor who played the older brother on
diff'rent strokes is arrested for shooting someone in a drug den in
south central los angeles the president or whatever of iran puts a
bounty on a writer you've never heard of right around the time you
start to think more about the author of the book that the movie you
liked was based on and you crank out a handful of short stories some
only a few pages long and show them to no one even though you'd
like to publish them as a book the last time you wrote something
your fifth-grade teacher typed it up for you offering editorial

suggestions and even helping you send it off to publishers in new york city most of them not responding but a few sending along form rejections the seriousness of the endeavor left an impression on you writing seemed like something that impressed adults but so did a million things one story you wrote a humorous piece for your high school girlfriend full of puns about having sex with her is found by her mother and you're not allowed to see her for a period of time even though you get an audition with the mother to plead that the story is fiction nothing but which seems to matter not the commercial pepsi paid madonna millions to make debuts during the cosby show but the next day the video madonna made for her song like a prayer debuts and the two side by side are a study in extreme contrasts suddenly christians are supposedly not drinking pepsi you talk the night manager of the fish and chips into cosigning for a car phone for your new ride you wouldn't dare ask your own parents and tread on the freewill parenting plus you know they'd say no the car phone is installed and you pretend to be talking on it whenever you pull in and out of the parking lot of the private school even letting a kid use it at recess the yellow-lit buttons lighting up with a satisfying beep when you turn the key in the ignition you're not sure if it's the phone or not but you inch into another group of private-school friends and when you're invited by the kid with the black mercedes to ditch and go see president reagan at arizona state university you agree and zip to tempe with the others in the black mercedes which you note has a car phone too a point you bring up casually you learn the others are all in a young republicans club which doesn't interest you until you learn it meets at the house of one of the girls at the neighboring private school and you agree to join them though you forget about it completely when you hatch a plan to join the mormon church in order to enliven the same stale route your relationship with your high school girlfriend is headed down unsure how else to keep the relationship going and also you have the sense that you'll probably get married or at least it'll come up soon because mormon girls start talking about marriage at a very young age and you know you can't

marry her unless you're mormon and so the math works out even
though math is not your strong suit but you never admit it is a stunt
even when your high school girlfriend prompts you to do so when
you start attending church regularly on sundays and again when you
arrange for meetings with the missionaries in her cousin's house
mostly so your parents won't find out you don't tell your friends
either and the enormity of the situation doesn't hit until you're wet
behind the ears having been dunked into the baptismal waters
standing at the pulpit in front of the crowd of mormon friends and
their families smiling up at you during the command performance
you give the attention welcome and familiar but the words coming
out of your mouth invented for the occasion forgotten before they're
uttered shortly thereafter a terrible thing happens to a jogger in
central park in new york city which is all the news can talk about
until it comes out that the actor rob lowe is in a sex tape everyone
wants to see but no one has any idea how you hardly have time to
practice your new mormonism before you graduate and move into
the tiny converted office in the one-bedroom apartment of your old
public-school friend who ripped up the carpets without the
landlord's consent and spray-painted the concrete floor black the
summer filled with parties put on by the foreign exchange club and
you heartily attend you feel like a fish out of water too just like the
college-aged foreigners far from home but you don't find kinship at
these parties mostly because the foreigners close ranks and you don't
blame them knowing it's for their own protection a television actress
from a show you've never heard of is murdered on her doorstep in los
angeles by a crazed fan from tucson and the papers drop the tidbit
that the actress became the object of the crazy's obsession when his
first obsession the girl from back east who wrote the letter to the
russian president died in that small plane crash and it seems weird
to share an obsession with a crazy person and you've never considered
that the false intimacy celebrity creates could be dangerous two
brothers in beverly hills murder their parents with shotguns in the
family tv room and try to convince the police that it's a mob hit

related to their record producer father's business but the police don't buy it and the brothers are ultimately arrested you put the fish and chips behind you for good when you accept a job as a runner for american continental corporation the parent company of lincoln savings and loan in california run by the already notorious charles keating jr who made national headlines when he tried to buy influence with a cadre of u.s. senators the clip of the question to charlie about whether or not he hoped to be buying influence and charlie's answer that he certainly hoped so a sound bite the press loves also the papers can't get enough of charlie or his lavish lifestyle his beautiful secretaries are referred to as charlie's angels and he lives in a mansion on the same property as his daughter and her husband parents of a kid who attends the same private school you barely graduated from the kid a nationally ranked swimmer and future olympian your job as a runner is to handle the phone calls and open the mail and rotate the company's fleet of mercedeses through the car wash and stock the supply rooms and fetch the catered lunches for the three floors of lawyers all working on the giant bankruptcy case charlie filed to protect himself and his assets from the federal government which has accused him of looting lincoln like it was his personal piggy bank not even the fall of the berlin wall or the fact that the u.s. government has noriega holed up in the vatican or that the mayor of washington dc is arrested for smoking crack or the pictures of the oil-drenched wildlife in alaska the result of the exxon valdez oil spill can distract the local headlines from charlie and his ongoing battle against the government old stories about charlie taking on larry flynt the publisher of the porn magazine hustler back when charlie was an antismut crusading prosecutor in his native cincinnati as well as newer stories about his calling former p.o.w. and arizona senator john mccain a wimp for not standing up to bank regulators on his behalf or the fact that all of the officers of american continental are related to charlie either by birth or by marriage a news truck is always parked out on the sidewalk in front of the american continental offices on camelback

road one time they pull into the driveway and you are sent to ask
them politely off the property which they do but not before asking
if they can interview you but even after only a month of working for
charlie you are in the cult and the idea repels you there's some
pleasure in denying the request charlie is summoned to washington
to testify before a committee about lincoln savings and loan and
when he takes the fifth the news goes wild and the phones in the
runners' room light up the mail full of indictments and threats the
one correspondent who faithfully sends a package every week with
epithets and pictures of his father who lost everything when lincoln
failed and took his own life the manila envelope like finding a
rattlesnake in the mailbag every time it appears when you actually
ask what it's all about people shrug and say that maybe elderly
investors in california were persuaded by lincoln employees to move
their savings from safe and guaranteed but low-interest accounts to
high-yield junk bonds so that charlie could then use the money to
build the lavish phoenician hotel at the base of camelback mountain
and for other purposes too the dispute seemingly is whether the
investors were greedy or the bank employees were illegally aggressive
and misleading no one will ever know the truth about that or the
rumor that the government blocked a sale of lincoln that charlie had
orchestrated which would've kept it from failing and from all those
people losing their money you don't see too much of charlie as his
office is up camelback road at the phoenician but one day you arrive
at the american continental offices and the parking lot is full of
moving vans the caravan idling among the clamor and whispers of
charlie's back and you learn that the government has seized the
phoenician and evicted charlie your sudden proximity to the boss is
invigorating and when you discover a box of yellow buttons that
proclaim i like charlie keating you wear them as part of your uniform
even on errands like the daily court filings downtown and the
airport runs for the cadre of lawyers from beverly hills charlie has
hired picking them up on mondays and dropping them off on fridays
the one lawyer the lead one telling you how much he regrets not

following his first love and becoming a veterinarian which you doubt because of the rolex on the lead lawyer's wrist you wear the button even when you're not working like the party at one of charlie's developer friends' estate where the pips are performing and you notice local celebrities like the center for the phoenix suns and the guy who reviews movies on television people look at you askance but in your heart of hearts you're doing it for the attention you couldn't care less about charlie or his problems but you like the association except when your high school girlfriend's mother bans you from the house because of your employment but by then you're skipping a lot of classes you camped out overnight to sign up for at the registrar's office your first college semester a nonevent and you're seeing even less of your high school girlfriend the ruse of attending church on sundays slipping too the whole enterprise coming apart though you can't see it just yet and when you take stock you apply the corrections suddenly finding your way to class and bombing back and forth between your apartment in tempe and the west side where you find places to meet your high school girlfriend outside of her house adjusting your shift at american continental to accommodate both always in transit and all facets of your life seem to be in a state of equilibrium until you wake up in time to see the metal bumper of the rusted suburban stopped at a red light you've somehow successfully driven off the freeway exit from another crosstown trip but you can't apply the brakes in time and the nose of your sports car the one you still owe many monthly payments on wedges under the metal bumper throwing you against your seat belt as the front of your car disappears the windshield cracking but the radio still blaring as you jump out and wait on the sidewalk to see what comes next that it's saturday night and your roommate can't be reached by the emergency room to come pick you up when you're diagnosed as being fine just a little shaken up and a lot sore is of less importance than the fact that your father warned you to renew your car insurance the previous friday so it didn't expire and it isn't until you're without it that you realize your car was the most important piece of the life you were living and without it everything is in doubt you can't get to work without catching two buses for a two-hour ride each way forget about trips to the west side to visit your high school girlfriend and the punch line is that without insurance you owe the total outstanding amount of your car loan immediately the answer to the vexing problem appears in the classified ads of the campus newspaper an ad about striking it rich working on a fish boat in alaska but the ad is really just to sell you a directory of 800 numbers for ships and canneries and you have to do the legwork but you plunk down the twenty bucks anyway and start making the long-distance calls from the switchboard at american continental after everyone else has left for the day all the jobs are taken have been promised since early in the semester but then one offers to hire you if you can be at sky harbor airport that night a ticket will be waiting for you at the counter and in a desperate few hours you call your high school girlfriend to tell her that you're leaving and have one of your fellow runners drive you to your apartment to pack a bag and then to a barbershop to have your head shaved quitting your job without notice your bewildered family and high school girlfriend meeting you at the airport that night when you say good-bye you have no idea when you'll return the first leg of the flight to salt lake city is like hurtling through a decompression chamber the stress of your recent problems releasing so that you fall into a deep sleep on the second leg from salt lake to anchorage alaska and with some solid sleep you realize that you might've made a huge mistake as you climb aboard the third leg the puddle jumper that will ferry you from anchorage to dutch harbor the village in the aleutian islands where your boat awaits the propellers on the puddle jumper are so loud you can't think and the cabin is cold and you try to stay focused on all the money you'll make enough to buy back things as they were the landing strip at the airport in dutch harbor is barely that the terminal not much more than a shack and the two norwegian fishermen sent by the ship to pick you up don't speak english so your panic-induced pantomime about a tragedy back home and how you must return immediately falls untranslated and after you receive the news that your bag hasn't come through you squeeze between the fishermen on the bench of the old ford pickup truck and cruise the harbor of ships gearing up for the sea the ships becoming smaller and smaller as you go until you reach yours the smallest among them and you're awarded a matching blue tracksuit with the words dutch harbor alaska stenciled in yellow down the right leg as clothes until your bag can be found you're instructed to help load the supplies stacked on the dock for the journey men of substance both fictional like jay gatsby and real like charlie keating have about them the myth of the self-made man and you buck in under this pretense the money earned over the summer will be more than you've ever made in your life and you'll use it as seed money to reinvent yourself when you return to phoenix a dream that is quickly deferred when the ship's captain tells you your job is not on the line where cutters who gut the day's catch are entitled to 1 percent of the haul each time the boat docks but in the kitchen as the cook's assistant and at an hourly wage significantly below what charlie keating was paying you the wood-paneled boat quickly becomes a floating tomb and you spend the first two days at sea in the cabin you share with the government inspector whose job it is to ensure that the boat is catching only the type of fish each season allows the windowless cabin enveloped in a fetid stench finally the captain appears in the swaying doorway to tell you that you need to start contributing and you spend all day in the galley working with the cook who plays the appliances tightly strapped to the counter like a maestro though the meals are marginally better than prison food albeit more plentiful you're surprised to learn that you're on trash duty which consists of grabbing up all the bags of trash and heaving them over the side of the boat the captain and crew sit at a wooden table on one side of the kitchen and the rest of you at another under the television wired to an old vhs machine the only two movies are teen wolf too and a mob movie with sean connery and dustin hoffman and matthew broderick and without wondering why and how the movies found their way on board you watch them in a heavy rotation during the downtime between meals when the cook rests in his cabin you run your hand over your shaven scalp to feel your hair growing back incrementally one of the cutters shatters the afternoon routine by appearing with a hook from one of the fishing nets caught in his ear a trickle of blood running into his yellow raincoat he asks you if you can pull the hook out and you tell him you don't think you can and he soldiers on to find someone who can help it quickly becomes apparent that you're to be relegated to the kitchen for the entire summer and when the captain tells you that you are also in charge of cleaning the bathrooms you haul in the power hose used to clean the fish guts off the line and douse the bathroom causing the drain to back up the captain livid a story you try to relay to your high school girlfriend on the ten-dollar-a-minute ship-to-shore phone calls that will come out of your paycheck along with the tracksuit you've been wearing day and night and when your high school girlfriend says maybe it's better if you stay for the entire summer you jump ship the moment the boat docks after two weeks at sea spending five of your last dollars on a cab ride from the ship to the airport leafing through a discarded people magazine about marlon brando's son murdering his sister's boyfriend while your father tries to get you a ticket on the last plane back to civilization which he does you're back home for a week or so before anyone knows you've returned and in your solitude you hit the books and do extensive research on your thesis that the mormon religion is completely made up by white men and stumble across a documentary called the god makers that proves the salient points of your argument armed with it you show up on your high school girlfriend's doorstep the look of surprise on her face the first clue that you are no longer welcome in her life but she lets you in and you present your case the look of surprise changing to a look of horror the god makers a known enemy propaganda and when you produce it begging her to watch it she asks you to leave and you do hearing through friends that she leaves that summer for an early start on her college career at brigham young university and you're overcome with the idea that you'll never see her again you ask for and get your job with charlie keating back some just assuming you were away on a two-week vacation though you're more weary than when you left the rest of the summer filled with news of the persian gulf war and worry among your friends about what will happen if the draft is reinstated some talk about fleeing to canada but it doesn't come to that the actor who played the older brother on diff'rent strokes is acquitted on manslaughter charges for the shooting in the drug den in south central los angeles you try to focus on your schoolwork as the new semester starts but just as school begins you get interested in writing television scripts and ferret out the advice that you should take a favorite tv show and write an original script on spec to use as a calling card the idea of moving to california to write for television immensely appealing you send away for a sample script for 21 jump street and then work on your own about a white supremacist modeled on a recent local news item involving a high school kid and his plans to kill minorities in churches and at schools which would be a perfect case for an episode of 21 jump street but the idea stalls on the page you take charlie keating to the airport in his custom mercedes so he can fly to los angeles and enter a plea in answer to the charges the state of california have made against him with regard to the failure of lincoln savings and loan with instructions to pick him up later in the day but you never see him again when the judge in california surprises him with a five-million-dollar bail he can't pay the controversial rap group 2 live crew is tried and acquitted on obscenity charges in florida stemming from a concert performance secretly recorded by two undercover police officers a few days before they're acquitted a federal judge declares their best-selling album obscene the government installs a trustee at american continental and a wave of charlie loyalists quit but you sense opportunity and agree to be one of the few runners who stay on the chaos at work is mirrored in the chaos of the atmosphere surrounding the national football league's unprecedented rescinding of the super bowl they previously awarded tempe when arizona voters reject an initiative to create a martin luther king jr holiday the loss of the super bowl means the loss of hundreds of millions of dollars and also black entertainers have called for a boycott of the state which loses more money the shadow of the used-car salesman governor lingering over the gubernatorial election that november which is billed as a fresh start but under the new laws meant to prevent a repeat of the election of the used-car salesman without a majority neither of the two new candidates receives a majority and a runoff election is scheduled for the spring the mayor in washington dc who got caught smoking crack in a hotel room and who has remained mayor all through his trial even running for reelection is sentenced to six months in prison a few days before the election which he loses the musical group milli vanilli are outed as lip-synchers and stripped of their grammy award which causes the kind of outrage found hardly anywhere else the date on the calendar when your ex-girlfriend returns from college for christmas break looms and when she readily agrees to see you you interpret that to mean that she's missed you as much as you have her but when you go into the windup of your apology for everything you've done and say words meant as a means to an end she so easily accepts them that you're taken aback and when she receives a phone call as if the moment is scripted her whispering into the phone it reveals the extent to which she's moved on from you and without explaining the interruption she lets you finish ghosts of your high school romance chase you away as you make a pleasant good-bye knowing you'll never ever see her again there's no one to share your pain with in that your parents and brothers never really knew her and your college friends have long forsaken your collective public school past for new adventures which you attempt to do by moving into the pink stucco apartment complex across the street from campus so notorious for partying everyone watching the war on television it looks like a video game you played as a kid you apply the same nonchalance to the start of the spring semester going stretches without showing up for class but making sure to attend the days of quizzes and tests your new volunteer job at the campus safety escort service keeps you on campus a little more you think it might be a good way to meet women since the girls who turn up at parties at your apartment complex are primarily interested in fraternity guys but you mainly escort married women to their cars after dark sometimes on foot and sometimes in a golf cart you and the other escorts race around campus in during downtime you continue to take two buses each way to your job working for the government trustee installed to wind down american continental and sell its assets for the benefit of its creditors your eyesight goes a little and you need glasses and even though you can't afford them you purchase a pair from the little optique in tempe because the girl behind the counter is cute she seems like she's flirting with you who can tell but on the chance that she might be you ask all the women you work with at american continental to vouch for you by writing the girl a note about you and how she should say yes when you ask her out you collect the notes and have them delivered and then call the girl seems genuinely flattered though she claims she has a boyfriend but agrees to a friend date you borrow your father's pickup for the date which is just dinner at chili's which goes okay you don't seem to have too much in common except your stunt and on the way to drop her back home you drive over a median you don't see because you suddenly realize you probably shouldn't be driving at night which freaks the girl out a little even though you make a small joke about adjusting the glasses you bought from her saying good night is the last time you'll see her you know the video for madonna's new song is banned from mtv and the guy on nightline asks her if she'll make even more money from the song now that it's banned madonna says yeah so what the harvard-educated businessman wins 2 percent above 50 in the runoff election and becomes governor but is immediately embroiled in litigation over his involvement with a different savings and loan from the one charlie owned the girl who played the sister on diff'rent strokes is caught robbing a video store in vegas where she is living and working at a dry cleaner's a girl at one of the parties at your apartment complex mistakenly dives into

the shallow end when she's drunk and comes up with a bloody face
and no one seems to know what to do everyone too drunk to drive
and you would offer but you don't have a car the girl from new jersey
who lives upstairs from you and who you think maybe likes you
from the road trip you made to mexico with her and her friends
offers to drive but the bloodied girl says she's fine and disappears
bret easton ellis the author of less than zero the book that the movie
you liked as a teenager was based on publishes a new book about a
stockbroker who is also a serial killer and his name is all at once
everywhere his handsome photo plastered all over the newspaper
and in magazines something about his original publisher canceling
the book over the violence and another publisher quickly cashing in
on the controversy which brings the author a slew of death threats
and his fame reignites your long-buried interest in becoming a
writer everyone watches the video tape of the rodney king beating
on television you are haunted by the image of the famous guitarist's
toddler son falling to his death out an open window in new york a
high school teacher in new hampshire is found guilty of ordering
one of her students who is also her teenage lover to murder her
husband warren beatty musing about how madonna doesn't exist if
there's no camera the kid from the partridge family who is a radio dj
in phoenix is found cowering in his apartment closet when the
police come to arrest him for beating up a transvestite prostitute
word is gangs from los angeles are infiltrating phoenix and a series
of shootings on the freeways seems to confirm the fact two shootings
in two weeks and then a third a pregnant woman rumor is
gangbangers are driving around at night with their lights off and if
you flash them to let them know they come after you so no one
flashes anyone after twenty years of marriage your parents decide to
divorce both of them young enough for a second act boxer mike
tyson is arrested for raping a beauty queen in a hotel room a man
running down the street in milwaukee with a handcuff on one arm
flags down police and he leads them to the apartment of the man
who tried to hold him against his will and the officers find an

apartment full of horrors you stop listening at the detail of four decapitated heads you stare at the photo of bennington college the school in a small town in vermont that bret easton ellis attended in the library's copy of peterson's guide to colleges and universities the tuition is outrageous it's one of the most expensive schools in the country and you become obsessed with transferring there the gradeless curriculum the answer to your drowning at a public university and when you ask your latin teacher for a letter of recommendation she reminds you that you're barely passing her class that summer pee-wee herman is arrested for masturbating in an adult theater in florida where he's been visiting his parents and the news explodes across all forms of media pee-wee goes into hiding his career ruined for what some deem hypocritical reasons but the jokes are funny unlike the joke made by the supreme court nominee about his coke can the television endlessly fascinated with the testimony of his former subordinate who claims she was sexually harassed by the nominee some people incredulous that the subordinate followed the nominee from job post to job post even after being harassed but she passes a lie detector and the nominee doesn't want to take one and on and on magic johnson arranges a press conference to announce that he is hiv positive and will retire from basketball immediately and as his team the lakers are perennial tormentors of the hometown phoenix suns some fans are not as compassionate as they could be magic goes on his friend arsenio hall's late-night show to assure everyone he is heterosexual and not gay which gets a standing ovation from the crowd lasting minutes you make the application to bennington college with the same conviction you're always able to muster when you want something to happen and you're momentarily elated when someone from the admissions office calls to request an interview which is the next step but even before you hang up you know you can't afford the flight to and from vermont especially because of the monthly payments for the car you'll never drive again and you reluctantly tell admissions this and they arrange for you to interview with a local alum a woman

who is a doctor in downtown phoenix you make an appointment
with her and then don't keep it and figure that's that a girl who
works with your college friend shows up at a party at your apartment
and while she likes your friend he has a girlfriend and so he wants
to introduce her to you and you hit it off immediately the fact that
she's still in high school no big deal at least to you but maybe a little
bit to her parents when you turn up at her house in scottsdale driving
the car your parents bought at an auction of old rental cars you start
spending all your time with your new high school girlfriend meeting
her friends who are also in high school the kick of being the oldest
in the group refreshing your outlook more than it should your new
high school girlfriend wants to be a writer too and that feels like a
real connection one you've never had before but you try not to make
too much out of it one of the kennedy relatives goes on trial for
raping a woman at the family compound in florida the movie about
jfk's assassination fires everyone's imagination especially those who
have been living with so many unanswered questions for so long and
for you and your friends it becomes the gospel truth about what
happened though others are quick to point out that it's simply
making an entertainment out of history but it's a compelling and
persuasive argument about the events from so long ago but also why
would all those famous people in the film agree to portray such
historical inaccuracies their celebrity lends a powerful credibility to
the whole thing and you check out every book in the phoenix public
library about marilyn monroe and her death hoping to unearth
some previously ignored kernel of information that solves the
mystery surrounding her demise but even though you keep the
books long past their due date you don't do more than leaf through
them looking at the pictures everyone watching a tv show on mtv
called the real world but you don't see much tv and don't have one
when you move into the cinder-block studio apartment in the
shadow of the pink stucco complex where you wasted time at so
many parties none of the faces becoming friends or names you can
remember there's a tv in the break room at american continental an

old back-projection big screen that you fire up during your lunch and where you learn about an extramarital affair committed by the democratic candidate for president the candidate going on 60 minutes with his wife to do damage control and also the boxer-who-raped-the-beauty-queen's trial and quick conviction the rich texan with the funny name and funny voice who announces his bid for the presidency on a nightly cable talk show even though he doesn't belong to either of the two traditional parties an allegedly new narrative some people get excited about but what little you know about politics doubts the texan is doing more than grandstanding especially when his candidacy is dependent on volunteers getting him on the ballot in every state which is a pretty good gimmick you have to admit the tennis player who contracted aids from a blood transfusion driving home after a late night with your new high school girlfriend it comes across the radio that the comedian sam kinison has been killed driving to las vegas just a few days after his wedding ceremony and it comes out later that a kid swerved across the lane and killed him and there's a rumor that the kid offers up his autograph for anyone who wants it not out of spite but because of his newfound fame charlie keating is sentenced by the state of california to ten years in prison and everyone says it's not a country-club prison but a real prison and he still has the feds to deal with but no one at american continental openly discusses charlie anymore especially the southern lawyer whose apprentice you've become you don't realize until much later how much you counted on becoming charlie keating's apprentice at least in terms of a meteoric rise but also because of the tales of charlie's previous lieutenants all of them making six figures a year to do charlie's bidding but all gone before you were hired the southern lawyer is much more grounded and less egomaniacal than charlie certainly or any of the other lawyers you've encountered he takes an interest in your academic work and rides you about it until you admit that you're not paying it the attention it deserves and you feel some shame about the fact for the first time all of american continental moves from its original compound on camelback road into half a floor of an office building a few blocks away and you agree to become the sole runner and switchboard operator so that the staff can be further downsized you also become a boy friday for the southern lawyer when he buys out of bankruptcy a mansion at the foot of camelback mountain formerly owned by a pair of nursing home administrators errands to home depot and letting contractors in to work you sometimes stay in the guesthouse on the property and you're allowed to use the pool anytime you watch a little of los angeles burning on the tv news borrow the southern lawyer's white mercedes given to him by american continental as one month's pay to take your new high school girlfriend and her friends to the prom staying in a hotel in downtown tempe near the mormon church on the asu campus whose wooden sign you recently destroyed in a drunken rampage when you learned that your mormon ex-girlfriend was getting married that summer a teenage girl on long island shoots but doesn't kill the wife of the guy who works on her car when she brings it in to his auto body shop the friend of the actor who played colonel hogan on one of your favorite shows as a kid hogan's heroes is arrested for colonel hogan's murder at an apartment complex in scottsdale the murder happening sometime in the late seventies long before you even started watching the show and you wonder at the complicit silence among the adults who knew that the actor had had his head bludgeoned in his sleep and possibly as a result of his sex life which included homemade pornographic movies and swinging and who knows what else the friend who is arrested all these years later was always the prime suspect and there's doubt that the evidence will stand up but the news repeats all the salacious details for those not in the know the summer is mostly spent at the southern lawyer's house running various errands and using the pool including some skinny-dipping with your new high school girlfriend and her friends the time you come over and the southern lawyer's current girlfriend is sunbathing nude you sneak back out the way you came but not immediately you continue your work as a boy friday for the southern lawyer to earn some spending money the southern lawyer tells you to bring a copy of your latest work you wonder at the motor home idling on the recently paved circular driveway a large group gathered under the awning filling their plates with food a fleet of rental cars parked two deep rings the motor home a miniature race car is parked where the southern lawyer's mercedes and land cruiser are normally parked and he motions you over and introduces you as the writer to someone who turns out to be the director of the film they're making at the southern lawyer's house the female lead a dark-haired woman in her thirties picks at a fruit salad while the male lead an englishman with a crew cut talks rabidly about the miniature race car he apparently brings with him on every location the director is not that interested in your writing it seems but he gives you his card telling the cast and crew five minutes while the southern lawyer excuses himself to make a phone call you follow the crowd up to the guesthouse which has been transformed into a movie set the sound guy having built a booth just outside the sliding glass doors inside a small camera track circles the queen-size bed the male lead motions for you to take a seat and asks you where you're from he sounds like james bond or at least to you and you tell him you're from montana originally the female lead brushes by in a red satin robe and you turn to the male lead to tell him a funny story about the mulching pit you built behind the guesthouse out of railroad ties but the male lead stands talking about his desire to travel to montana while he slips out of his clothes and it becomes obvious what kind of film they're shooting in the guesthouse though you're surprised by the elaborate production the female lead points at you and says that it's a closed set and so you don't see a thing searching the main house for the southern lawyer but he has for the moment disappeared as does the director's card before you can send him some of your work which oddly you're interested in following through on you promise yourself you're going to spend more time on your classes this go around but your new high school girlfriend means a lot of late nights especially the ones where she sneaks out of her house and so your grades fall off a cliff immediately and are on life support the rest of the way just like your finances so you take a night job manning the desk of the campus law library helping people look up statutes but mostly just reshelving books pulled down by law students too absorbed to reshelve them you lay your hands on madonna's sex book the moment it goes on sale at the local barnes & noble the large-format book with metal covers and spiral binding comparatively tame to what you know about madonna and you give the book to the southern lawyer who wants to give it to a conservative friend as a gag gift you hammer out a couple of short stories including one about a polygamist mormon and his three wives arizona voters approve a statewide holiday for martin luther king jr and are rewarded when the national football league awards the state the right to host the super bowl three years on the actor who played the older brother on diff'rent strokes is arrested when he's pulled over by police who find drugs and a loaded gun the dream of becoming a writer finally trumps all else and you leave the aftermath of the collapse of charlie keating's empire behind and tempe and arizona state university and your old high school girlfriend too and move ninety miles south to the university of arizona to finish your undergraduate degree in their creative writing program taking an apartment just off campus down park avenue which you think is funny you have no furniture no car hardly any money save for what's left over in student loan aid after each semester's tuition but the redbrick campus has a unifying effect and for the first time in your short academic career school becomes the main focus your new high school girlfriend visits a couple of times on the greyhound bus but you both sense that the relationship has run its course no hard feelings charlie keating is convicted again this time by the federal government michael jackson appears on oprah winfrey's talk show and claims to have a skin disease and that he doesn't bleach his skin like some claim a truck bomb explodes at the world trade center doesn't do what it's supposed to knock one building into the other but it does kill a handful of people the actor who played the older brother on diff'rent strokes is arrested for stabbing a guy renting a room from him when he tells the guy to quit yelling at his girlfriend but he's later cleared when the stabbing turns out to be self-defense the little kid from diff'rent strokes everyone loved wins a lawsuit against his parents who squandered all the money he made the actor son of the famous martial artist is killed on a movie set when a blank is fired at him same as it was jon-erik hexum years before you aim to model your writing career primarily on bret easton ellis's since he is a young and famous writer and you want that too so you begin work on your first novel called the vegetable king which loosely resembles a mash-up of fitzgerald's the great gatsby and bret easton ellis's american psycho the television in the student union plays the raid at the waco compound on a loop everyone gathered around as if it's homework a tennis player is stabbed during a tournament and at first people assume it's because of her nationality but really the stabber is just a fan obsessed with the player's rival the campus literary magazine wants to publish your short story about the polygamist leaving a note on your door about it since you don't have a phone tucson empties when summer arrives and you work eight hours a day on your novel sometimes treating yourself to the dollar movie on campus regardless of quality or to an hour in front of the television in the student union where you watch news unfold incrementally prince changes his name to a symbol and nobody knows what to call him the woman in beverly hills who is arrested for running a prostitution ring involving celebrity clients the white house lawyer whose body is found in a park dead from suicide something to do with the real estate scandal involving the president that no one seems to know the specifics of the boy whose father accuses michael jackson of molestation though it might just be a shakedown basketball superstar michael jordan's father going missing his body turning up in a swamp a couple of weeks later the menendez brothers' trial broadcast minute by minute on a cable channel the two dressed in colored sweaters to make them look not like the kind of kids who could level shotguns at their parents you also kill some of the summer at the free wine receptions at the poetry center which is just a little house on cherry street where you hear some great writers including a graduate fiction writer whose first story was published in esquire magazine because the esquire editor happened to be subbing in for the instructor who was his wife and the graduate student's story happened to be up for workshop that day a lucky story that gives you great energy and hope and by the fall you have a finished version of your novel it takes a week to print it out though because you don't have a printer and the monitors in the campus computer labs are tight about how many pages anyone can print at once so you put the different labs on a loop knowing when the monitors change posts so that you can print out a copy of the entire novel which you mail straight off to random house the biggest publisher and the one who publishes your idol every admirer is one part assassin you spend a lot of time wondering what random house thinks of your book while golfing a tennis ball into cups you've set up in your barren living room the golf clubs formerly belonged to your friend who looked like anthony michael hall and you were always meaning to return them and when you finally did after your friend shot himself in the head his mother said he'd want you to keep them even though what she was saying was that she didn't want them in the house you're tapped as the fiction editor for the campus literary magazine and in turn ask a girl in your creative writing class to be the coeditor and she agrees and you set to work on the slush pile trying to make fair judgments on the work submitted a job you come to appreciate as next to impossible though it doesn't assuage your disappointment when a ups deliveryman shows up on your door with a package from random house you momentarily think contains a contract and a check why else would they send it ups but really just contains the copy of your manuscript and a letter saying thanks but no thanks the fibers from your ripping open the ups envelope catching in your carpet and without a vacuum cleaner you have no way to clean them up the actress winona ryder offers a large reward for the little girl from ryder's hometown who is kidnapped from a slumber party your friend from maryland who is as much a fitzgerald fan as you tells you that river phoenix died outside a nightclub in hollywood owned by johnny depp and while there seems to be an insinuation in these facts it's just a terribly sad thing that happened the girl in your apartment complex who tells you the dirty joke you don't understand until much later has a copy of the rob lowe sex tape and shows it to you and after all the years of hearing about it and even the coy allusions to it in that movie rob lowe made as a comeback after the scandal the video of what happened in the hotel room at the democratic national convention in atlanta years previous is tame and a little boring the body of the little girl from winona ryder's hometown who was kidnapped from a slumber party is found your friend the fitzgerald fan goes to the inaugural insomniyakathon with you twenty-four hours of readings at a bar in tucson which you consider a pretty genius gimmick not unlike the entire career of howard stern the dj in new york whose book sells out in a matter of hours with millions more sold thereafter the book signings like carnivals with people in costumes and it seems like stern will say just about anything but you sort of get that he's doing it to do it and it wouldn't be outside the realm of possibility that it's all an act but even more curiously the book seems to be a springboard to movies and television deals stern is on everyone's lips the novelty of so many people who wouldn't normally be reading books suddenly reading one seems only a mockery stern stages a pay-per-view new year's eve special called the miss howard stern new year's eve pageant where women do things like eat maggots and put plastic bags over their heads and while the special grosses a ton of money hollywood executives who have been considering stern for the job of replacing chevy chase as a late-night host change their minds and so too do movie executives interested in bringing some of stern's ideas to the screen an olympic skater is attacked whacked in the knee and it turns out to be a hit ordered by her rival skater your application to be an intern at the university of arizona press is granted and your curiosity about the publishing side of writing brims and maybe they'll even want to publish your novel but after a

week it's clear the press doesn't publish books like yours and really
doesn't publish much fiction and while the different phases editorial
layout cover art publicity are interesting the internship becomes a
thing around your neck and you don't get credit for the class when
you don't write the final paper about your experience as required
radio personality howard stern announces his candidacy for the
governor of new york madonna is a guest on david letterman's show
and her appearance has to be heavily edited to be shown diane
sawyer is sitting in for your favorite news anchor peter jennings and
the words coming out of her mouth on the television given to you by
your parents cannot possibly be true but it's all over all the other
channels too the lead singer of the band nirvana is dead of a suicide
in the room over the garage in his house and the facts and rumors
and lies about the story consume everyone you know for days and
weeks a woman sues the president claiming he sexually harassed her
in a hotel room when he was governor of arkansas the issue of the
campus literary magazine you helped edit comes out you and your
coeditor agreeing to disagree about a postmodern story you want to
include just to have one even though it's subpar compared with some
other realist fiction stories submitted something about the variety
appealing to your nascent editorial sense rumor has it that kojak's
son is a student at the university of arizona and that his girlfriend
tori spelling has been seen around tucson and that tori spelling's
castmate from 90210 jennie garth is from phoenix which matters to
devotees of the show you've never seen it though you know all of the
characters' names the rumor that you just need to take the university's
math placement test in order to have a score of some kind to then be
admitted to math x a class for artists and writers that satisfies the
university's math requirement for graduation turns out not to be
true a fact you learn only after you've breezed in and out of the test
penciling in random answers based on your test score you won't be
graduating that december as planned because you need two years of
math classes to reach the class you need for credit the test score
locking you in also you're so derelict about your studies that while

you know you need latin 202 to complete your foreign-language credit you fail to see the obvious that it's only offered in the spring and not between now and when you're supposed to graduate so you make sure you're the first to sign up for the summer class even though the lease on your apartment is up at the end of may you intended to go back to phoenix for the fall semester arranging all your classes on tuesdays and thursdays with the idea of attending just on tuesdays to save the money you don't have for an apartment but the more pressing problem is the college algebra class there's really no point in taking the summer latin class if you can't solve the college algebra problem the answer is found the week after oj simpson murders his wife and her friend and then leads the police on a slow freeway chase a mailer for a brand-new community college opening in phoenix arrives in the mail and almost as a dare you call the number on the mailer to ask if you can enroll in college algebra and to your astonishment the voice on the other end takes your credit card information and just like that you're enrolled in the monday/wednesday/friday fall college algebra class at the new community college oj simpson offers a $500,000 reward for information leading to the arrest of the real killer or killers of his wife and her friend radio personality howard stern withdraws from the race for governor of new york rather than publicly reveal his financial statements all of the apartments in tucson are sublet for the summer and after multiple dead ends you scour the dorms on campus for any last-minute cancellations and find luck in that a group of native mexicans enrolled in a summer language immersion class at the university have some missing students and you're given a bunk in a white cinder-block room with a guy who speaks no english but seems good natured enough you never see each other you can't stomach the cramped quarters which remind you too much of your room on the alaskan fish boat and though you don't have any money or a car you find ways to be out of the room either going to dollar movies or walking the halls of the air-conditioned buildings on campus or reading in the library or browsing the new books and magazines in the campus bookstore where you spot the new issue of vanity fair with the article titled who's afraid of bret easton ellis all about what the author has been doing since his controversial book was published a few years earlier and also announcing the publication of his new book a story collection called the informers and even though you can't afford it you buy the magazine so you can read and reread the piece and stare at the caricature drawn of the author you can't afford the new story collection but read it surreptitiously in the campus bookstore you can't make much of it but who are you to judge you write a letter to the editor of vanity fair in support of the author's place in contemporary fiction not sure why but probably mostly because if they print it maybe ellis will see it your last college semester begins and you live ninety miles away so you can concentrate on your monday wednesday friday college algebra class at the new community college on the west side of phoenix you living back home your father dropping you at sky harbor airport on monday nights so you can grab the shuttle to tucson for your other classes on tuesdays you bunk on the couch of your old high-school-aged girlfriend who has just started after a year of community college back in phoenix it's the first time you have any kind of relationship with an ex-girlfriend and there's something dependable about a friendship with someone who knows you so well and you begin to look forward to those nights they break up your otherwise monastic existence the bad reviews for bret easton ellis's book start rolling in and you're not sure why but you write a letter to the editor of entertainment weekly in response to one of the harsher reviews and to your surprise they print it the thrill of your name in the magazine matched only by the message on the answering machine at home that vanity fair is going to print your letter as well the stars aligning when you happen upon a flyer on the fourth floor of the modern languages building on campus where all your creative writing workshops are held for a new low-residency mfa program at bennington college you take in the news stunned a little and then steal the poster so that no one else sees it before you can get your application in you include your latest short story written from the ashes of your failed novel your favorite creative writing professor told you after class that it was probably a publishable story and so you spent an afternoon licking envelopes and stamps to mail it off to all the literary magazines listed in the back of the latest best american short stories collection the book your professor used in class there's a lot of hope and optimism the federal government grinds to a halt and shuts down something you didn't know could even happen though the finger-pointing is less of a surprise former president ronald reagan announces that he has alzheimer's the last the public hears from him one night a few weeks before your december graduation you're out at the pool in your ex-girlfriend's apartment complex and it strikes you that you have no alternative plan should you not get into bennington that you should've applied to a handful of places arrogance isn't to blame you just aren't interested in pursuing the course of study if it isn't at bennington in the shadow of bret easton ellis the coming new year is a blank slate you have no idea where you'll be living what you'll be doing for work nothing the vacuum created by the absence of any kind of schooling too frightening to contemplate vanquished by the phone call from the director of the mfa program who calls during dinner to tell you that you've been accepted and will start in january and then more great good luck the editor of one of the literary magazines in new york city you mailed your story to sends a handwritten note in pencil saying they're considering publishing it so that by the time of your graduation from the university of arizona please stand and turn your tassel along with thousands of others congratulations good-bye your life as a graduate student and possibly a published author has begun you gather your father and two brothers under the same roof in a rented house in a master-planned development in phoenix built around a large man-made lake the first time you've been in the same house in you can't remember how long there's no money to furnish the five-bedroom pink stucco house as it should be but everyone has their living space and you use the extra room as a writing office you're so eager to start your first ten-day residency of the low-residency mfa program at bennington college that you take a red-eye to albany not realizing that you'll have to wait until dawn to hire a driver to take you to the secluded campus in the woods of vermont the slatted sunshine its own miracle as you are expelled from the covered bridge at the foot of campus which is deserted at this time of the morning you survey the landscape you've seen only in pictures the red barn structure that houses the administration the white seventies-style architecture of crossett library the clock-towered commons at the head of the enormous lawn buried under crisp snow that runs out to the end of the world so named because the lawn drops off like a runway your vision taking flight over the green mountains green-and-white clapboard dorms line the lawn and you wonder which one bret easton ellis lived in eager to commune with his ghost you set your bag down on a picnic table and scan the horizon for signs of anyone else bret easton ellis probably sat at this picnic table you think you let yourself into a near dorm all the doors unlocked it seems and think bret easton ellis probably partied in this common room and as your head hits the pillow in an unlocked room the first real sleep since you left phoenix you wonder if he even perhaps lived in the very room you're in it's a possibility until you learn otherwise when you awake dazed to the sound of clanging heaters you get your correct room assignment and scurry off to the welcome reception in the commons disappointed that most of the other writing students have not heard of bret easton ellis or the ones who have just smile talk revolves around the poet robert frost or the writer bernard malamud both dead and lionized and decidedly not very interesting the next day after breakfast served in the commons at communal tables with your fellow students and most of the writing instructors you wander as a lark into the alumni office and tell the girl working the counter that you're a student and want the address of an alum the girl seems skeptical since all the undergraduate students are away in january for winter break and after some discussion with her boss about whether or not mfa students have the same privileges as other students she writes bret easton ellis's address and phone number on a yellow post-it note and hands it across the desk you vamoose before she can recall the information securing the post-it in your wallet after memorizing the address in case the post-it somehow gets lost fresh from victory you head to the library and search the computer for ellis's books and learn that the library has on deposit ellis's student thesis called this year's model which you don't immediately recognize as a song title by elvis costello but you do recognize some of the stories from the thesis as those from ellis's latest collection the informers you also put a request in for the thesis of ellis's classmate donna tartt whose novel the secret history you loved tartt dedicated the book to ellis for helping her and for recommending her to his literary agent which you hope he'll do for you too you fall in love with the other writing students the feel of immediate family permeating the workshops and lectures you volunteer to organize some student readings and choose the laundry room as a suitable venue when no other can be secured the laundry room readings becoming something of a legend severe separation anxiety overcomes you as you board your flight back to phoenix the resumption of your life akin to coming to periscope depth oj simpson's trial for murdering his wife and her friend begins in los angeles you need a job and gravitate toward the camelback corridor where you worked for charlie keating at american continental and randomly put in an application at the family print shop near the old american continental offices remembering how you and the other runners pitched in to buy flowers for the stunning girl who worked the counter the one time someone at american continental wanted some color copies from the print shop the girl had tattoos which you normally didn't care for but she was flirty and it was enough to spring for the bouquet the card signed simply the runners at acc when you get the job at the family print shop running the xerox machines you relay the story to your boss and he remembers it the girl was his girlfriend and the story suddenly doesn't seem so funny though the girlfriend is long gone the print shop is a boon in terms of your being able to photocopy your work for sending off to literary magazines and to the teacher assigned to you by bennington for the semester a writer you've never heard of but whose book you buy with the intention of reading it the literary magazine in new york city that was considering publishing your story writes to say they're accepting it for publication and you pin the acceptance on the wall above your desk next to the yellow post-it note with ellis's address and phone number one of the customers at the print shop runs a mail-order russian bride business and you leaf through the yearbook of women he prints thinking a bunch of different thoughts at once another customer is the daughter of the famed russian ballet dancer vaslav nijinsky whom you've never heard of but you come to learn his life's story as the daughter is working on a book about her father and when she arrives at the print shop you know the next hour or two will be spent helping her copy old news clippings and photos you gather that nijinsky was famous for being the only male ballet dancer who could perform on his tiptoes like you saw michael jackson do on that motown special when you were in grade school everyone wowed by the new dance jackson called the moonwalk you play a practical joke on the good-natured designer who works at the print shop an admitted and avowed marijuana smoker you conspire with your boss who has become one of your closest friends to announce upon the designer's return from his marijuana-fueled honeymoon that the print shop is switching health insurance companies and everyone has to take a drug test you go down to the arizona department of health services claiming to be a college kid doing a research project and in need of a drug test kit the department of health services worker tells you that he can give you the forms and cup but that he has to write the word void across the forms which he does and which is no problem as you and your boss re-create them back at the print shop the designer learns about the test and confides in you that he's going to run out at lunch to buy a masking agent at a smoke shop which he does but back at his desk the masking agent makes him defecate involuntarily and he has to go home for the day the practical joke taking on a life of its own the designer takes the drug test the next day and when your boss tells him he's failed it and his only option is to enroll in drug classes the designer's face gets red and he says no way he's taking classes but that night his wife lets him know that he will in fact have to take the classes so when he comes to work again his face a little hangdog he accepts that he has to take the classes and you and your boss stop the whole thing before it can go any further and the designer is relieved but his wife is angry and calls your boss and gives him an earful oj's houseguest tells about going to mcdonald's with oj the limo driver meant to take oj to the airport rang the doorbell repeatedly before oj appeared looking sweaty the guy tricked into meeting his secret admirer for an episode of the jenny jones show learns the secret admirer is a man and murders the admirer a few days after the show the singer selena is murdered by her assistant who it turns out was stealing money from her the newscaster refers to her as the mexican madonna someone blows up a truck in front of the federal courthouse in oklahoma the galleys for your first short story arrive from the literary magazine in new york city and you stare at them in disbelief your words arranged by an unseen editorial hand three thousand miles away the daughter of actor marlon brando whose brother murdered her husband commits suicide a forensic specialist testifies that the odds against the dna found at the crime scene being anyone else's but oj simpson's are astronomical the actress who played samantha on bewitched dies of cancer the actor who played superman is thrown off his horse and paralyzed from the neck down you spin in circles at an old ice-packing plant in downtown phoenix while former porn star traci lords plays music in her new incarnation as a dj summer in vermont is hotter than you expected but your second residency is made uncomfortable not by the heat but by the secret knowledge you've been carrying that you didn't do the work prescribed by the program between residencies not because you weren't eager but because the writer assigned as your mentor quit responding to your monthly packets and so you quit mailing them all of which is exposed when the writer is fired rumors about a divorce hampering his teaching and it emerges that the other students assigned to the writer had the same experience as you and you're called to account with the administration who threaten not to give you credit for the first semester which is a problem because you're on financial aid and can borrow only so much money surely not for extra future semesters the mercurial irishman who directs the program and whom you once considered an ally seems like the head instigator in your not getting credit the whole thing a cloud over you upsetting because you were so looking forward to seeing everyone again after living your surface life in phoenix but one of the other authors who teach workshops hears of your plight and then something happens that you never really understand and the matter drops with the caveat that you'll have to do two times the work in the upcoming semester and you agree and get on with the residency working late into the nights on the daily fake newsletter some of the students conspire to publish contributing a column under the byline m not fitzgerald late nights at the end of the world under tiki torches you lacquered in bug spray an endless can of beer in your hand sweaty dances in the carriage barn or in the tiny pub on campus flipping through a copy of details magazine in the air-conditioning of crossett library you find a profile of the actor val kilmer by bret easton ellis and feel an electricity of stumbling across ellis's name while being on campus a continuous circle of a kind photos of oj simpson's wife and friend in rivers of blood on the saltillo tile of your youth are all over the news oj tries on the bloody glove a police officer found on oj's property but the glove appears not to fit one of charlie keating's lieutenants is discovered in the early morning in his lexus parked in the parking lot of a toy store a bullet in his brain a few days later another of charlie's lieutenants does the same in his home a handsome actor whose movies you haven't seen is arrested for soliciting a prostitute in los angeles the world agog as the handsome actor's girlfriend is a world-renowned model and actress screen legend lana turner dies a couple of days later but the handsome actor and the prostitute dominate the news oj's doctor says he's too hobbled from football injuries to be able to commit a double homicide but a recent videotape of oj working out while touting an arthritis remedy counters that you read a handful of short stories each week as makeup work and begin writing as many short stories of your own as you can to put yourself back even with the administration at bennington a north carolina judge blocks oj's lawyers' attempt to force a screenwriter who interviewed the police officer who found the incriminating glove for background on a screenplay she was writing to testify to the fact that the police officer is a racist you write a story about a narrator who visits the small town where he was born and finds himself surrounded by racists the north carolina court of appeals grants oj's lawyers the right to hear the tapes of the screenwriter interviewing the police officer you write a twenty-page story that's all dialogue a phone conversation between a man and a woman the news is infatuated with pictures of oj wearing a famous brand of shoes like those that left prints at the crime scene you write a story about a stranger visiting his friend and abusing his friend's girlfriend in some indeterminate way the tapes of the screenwriter interviewing the police officer are played in court but not in front of the jury the officer is heard using the n word constantly contrary to his own previous testimony that he never used it the police officer swiftly invokes his fifth amendment rights there's some debate about whether or not newspapers should publish a rambling antigovernment manifesto by the unabomber a terrorist the government has been after for years the unabomber promises more bombing if the manifesto isn't published in the new york times and the washington post oj simpson applies to trademark his name standing in line at the grocery store getting groceries for you and your father and brothers you pick up details magazine and flip to the last page which features two blond girls posing and giving short answers to a q and a and you can't tell what they do or why they're in the magazine and you come away with the idea that their sole purpose as a quote-unquote group is to become famous and you consider how weird the concept is that someone could be celebrated for just being celebrated and you write an eight-page story called we're so famous around the idea everyone gathered around the small television on top of the xerox machine at the family print shop when they announce the verdict in the matter of the people v oj simpson which you're convinced will be guilty and something akin to shock sets in when it's otherwise and you contemplate for the first time really how much mental energy you expended on the narrative even though you had no stake in the outcome personally a feeling like fatigue settling over you in the following weeks and months as everyone traipses around either in elation or frustration you're all the way back in the good graces of the administration at bennington when the january residency begins you can't believe you're halfway through graduate school when bret easton ellis was your age he'd published two novels and was working on his third the one that would make him famous all over again an unused part of the campus has been rented by a shakespearean theater company so unknown faces known to be aspiring thespians turn up in the dining hall from time to time the one next to you in line complaining about the dining hall running out of strawberries for strawberry shortcake turns out to be the actress raquel welch you make a sympathetic remark about the strawberries before you recognize her but she doesn't seem to hear you madonna reluctantly testifies in court against the man who broke into her hollywood home and threatened to slice her up if she didn't become his wife we've made his fantasies come true madonna admonishes the court which compelled her to testify sitting right in front of him instead of by videotape or some other method one way to meet a celebrity on your terms one of the producers who made all the big movies of the eighties like flashdance beverly hills cop and top gun is found dead in his bathroom from a drug overdose and there are whispers that a botched penile implant is to blame magic johnson comes out of retirement to play for the lakers the hard contacts you've been wearing don't seem to be working and your eye doctor tells you that you have a condition that causes your corneas to elongate weakening at the tip and you'll need a corneal transplant to correct the problem you get on the waiting list for a donated cornea your case different from most in that you need a relatively young cornea and so you're essentially waiting for someone your age or younger to pass away the procedure is outpatient you're awake during it though they put you under to drug up the eye and then bring you back so you can alert them to any problems but it all goes smoothly and your eye doctor tells you seriously not to get into any pillow fights or allow any kind of trauma to your eyes and you wonder how you're going to get through life without violating that mandate howard stern announces that he'll star in the film version of his own book to the delight of his fans the rapper snoop dogg is arrested for allegedly murdering a rival gang member the summer before the arrest taking place after snoop presents an award at the mtv music awards you keep your head down reading and writing in the little office above the garage in the house you're sharing with your father and two brothers enjoying being under the same roof even though you're all living your own lives your youngest brother attending the local high school your other brother and father working everyone home most nights for the dinner you prepare trying to learn how to cook a month or so after your corneal transplant the eye doctor tells you to lean forward and keep your eye open so he can begin removing the tiny stitches your friend from bennington's husband is an actor traveling with a play coming to gammage auditorium in tempe and you offer to put him up he looks like christopher reeve which he gets a lot especially after the accident you see the play with one of your friends who you can tell has an immediate crush on him but he probably gets that a lot too the play goes to los angeles and you and your friend from your charlie keating days drive out to see the actor and his wife your friend from bennington staying with them in the old fifties hotel converted into apartments filled with struggling actors the kidney-shaped pool at the center of the tahitian-themed complex going unused you love the idea of all the little compartments filled with ambitious people trying to realize their dream and feel a sort of kinship even though back in phoenix you continue to keep your head down don't date don't see your old friends who have all scattered here and there no one believes the story the menendez brothers tell about the abuse they suffered at the hands of their father and they're found guilty of murder don't eat meat or you'll catch mad cow disease charlie keating's conviction is overturned and he's released the unabomber is arrested when his brother recognizes the rantings of the manifesto published in the newspapers as those of his crazy brother living in the woods in montana the rapper mc hammer files for bankruptcy and you think man where did all that money go the actress from the superman movies is found hiding in some bushes in a suburb of los angeles with all her hair cut off and ranting she was apparently in the bushes for days you spend what time you do spend socializing with the manager of the family print shop who has unexpectedly become your closest friend the def leppard drummer with one arm is arrested for choking his wife for a small fee you can purchase a vhs tape directly from oj with his side of the story but no one seems to want it the summer residency at bennington is the penultimate residency for you and you feel a mild panic about what will happen to you after you graduate you can't imagine hanging on any longer in phoenix you never felt at home there always a double life and now you have the vocabulary to express it but you also can't imagine leaving your family a vexation you express to one of your mentors on a walk through the woods at bennington and he encourages you to do what you feel is right but you think easy for him to say though you never really know if your family's dependence on you is real or imagined the host of the family feud game show is found hanging in the closet of a hospital where he went for mental observation one of the best customers at the family print shop a psychiatrist with an office in downtown phoenix shoots himself through the heart with a handgun you can't stop thinking about how he must've been alive for a few minutes right after the actor who portrayed one of the leads in the film version of bret easton ellis's first novel less than zero is arrested for being under the influence of drugs and then arrested again a couple of weeks later when he's found asleep in a bedroom of the house next door to his assault charges against the old guy who played colonel potter on the television show m*a*s*h are dropped after he completes an anger management course for beating his seventy-year-old wife the year before fans of the rock group van halen are overjoyed when the original front man returns but his second tenure is brief an all-girl band from england records a song that blares from every speaker and the interesting fact is that the band was manufactured as an answer to all the boy bands in pop music different from the usual origin story about a couple of musicians inviting others to join them in starting a band this group was culled from hundreds of applicants who answered a small ad in london a sheep not born but cloned is introduced to the world a jetliner filled with passengers headed to paris and then rome explodes just after takeoff from new york and the television is filled with pictures of burning debris floating in the ocean some eyewitnesses allege seeing a missile fired into the jetliner a bomb explodes at the olympics in atlanta and the eyewitness who is at first hailed as a hero is then arrested as the chief suspect and vilified in the press as a lonely wannabe the singer rick james is released from prison after serving time for assault everyone is trying to guess who alanis wrote the song about your high school friend whose sister you briefly dated in high school is murdered in the parking lot of an after-hours club in scottsdale in the police account a kid pulled a gun on your friend and his friends and your friend said you're not going to shoot me but then the kid with the gun did you think back to when you last saw your friend at a grocery store in phoenix buying something for his infant daughter and you feel ashamed that you tried to avoid him but he found you in an aisle anyway and you tried to catch up a little remember the old days you having no plausible explanation for what you were up to only because you were hedging about the fact that you had a foot in two worlds and were conflicted about making the leap everyone doing the macarena at the democratic national convention the rapper tupac shakur is shot in las vegas after attending a boxing match miraculously the letter you wrote to bret easton ellis asking to interview him for your graduate lecture at bennington which is to be a recitation of your literary journey to date is answered your father telling you that someone named bret left a message on the machine and when you return it ellis invites you to come to new york to conduct the interview in person and you immediately agree to the plan tupac holds on for almost a week before dying rumors that he's faked his own death abound the mother in texas who hired a hit man to kill her daughter's cheerleading rival's mother in an effort to get the rival to drop out of contention is sentenced to prison the mississippi review a small but prestigious literary magazine run by the acclaimed writer frederick barthelme accepts your short story we're so famous for publication the story chosen for the prize issue judged by mary robison another acclaimed writer and the feeling that having published one previous short story was a fluke recedes a little denied a seat at the presidential debates ross perot goes on larry king afterward to rebut the detective who found the bloody glove on oj's property enters a no-contest plea over his lying about not having used the n word in a decade or more in prepping for your interview with bret easton ellis you call the exclusive private school ellis attended to request any info and before you can say ellis's name the woman who answers the phone assumes you're calling about the actor matthew perry you arrive in new york city a day before your scheduled interview with ellis landing at your bennington friend's apartment in queens amazed to find yourself in a place you never thought you'd be the cacophony makes you giddy the landmarks you previously viewed only through the lens of a television screen or imagined from the pages of books big as the sun up close you scope out ellis's apartment in the east village too anxious about the interview but overprepared too you arrive early the next day with your tape recorder and notebook too early and you're made to wait in the lobby but then you realize you have to pee and the doorman points you in the direction of a bathroom down a hall and you start to worry that ellis will come looking for you and find you in the bathroom meant for the maintenance crew but when you return to the lobby the doorman tells you that you can go up and you didn't consider that ellis wouldn't in fact descend to the lobby to retrieve you the ride to the second floor is quick and when you land the elevator opens on a small hallway ellis's door slightly ajar and before you know it the shy author is shaking your hand and inviting you into his brightly lit but sparsely furnished loft there's no table and so you use a third chair for the tape recorder and the question-and-answer session lasts all afternoon and into the fading light you're astonished at the depth of his answers and your admiration for him grows tenfold he walks out with you when it's over to fetch some corona and limes from the corner deli and when you part he tells you that new york city is a great place to be a writer and it all but seals the matter in your mind bill clinton is the first democratic president since franklin roosevelt to win reelection michael jackson's longtime friend who is also a nurse in jackson's dermatologist's office is pregnant with his child and they quickly marry prince now wants to be called the artist a pint-size beauty queen is found murdered in her home right around christmas and no one seems to know who did it your last residency at bennington begins amidst the january snow with an incident involving a drunken student sexually harassing one of your poet friends so that you have to intervene not knowing the residency will degrade further from there after the student is asked to find accommodations off campus which he does at his in-laws' house your journey from the midnight showing of less than zero to the alma mater of bret easton ellis culminates with your lecture about said journey you hand out a lengthy xerox of the full q and a of your interview with ellis courtesy of the family print shop back in phoenix and deliver your graduating lecture in the subterranean auditorium known as tishman the doors clattering when you reach the part of your lecture about why and how ellis's notorious novel american psycho was

canceled by its publisher when some of the more violent passages are
leaked to the media only to be published by a rival publisher you
read one of the violent passages as an example your friends alerting
you to the fact afterward that some people walked out when you
began reading the passage you just shrug thinking whatever but
then a chain of letters appears on the bulletin board in the campus
mail room decrying your having read the passages out loud and you
get a little taste of the kind of controversy that surrounds ellis's
novel but so what but then someone posts a letter about burning
your handout of the q and a and the campus erupts in a first
amendment controversy that has you looking over your shoulder
and hiding in your dorm room the faculty silent on the matter
mostly you think because it involves ellis and not a writer they care
about each day more terrible than the next in terms of rumors about
what you've done you call ellis and tell him what's happening and he
just laughs and says it doesn't surprise him and you adopt his cool
attitude while trying to dodge karen finley the artist who was one of
a handful who notoriously had their nea artist grants vetoed on the
grounds of subject matter she and the other artists sued and won but
the end result was the nea folded ending grants to artists someone
on the faculty tries to arrange a summit between you and finley but
the idea embarrasses you and you avoid her successfully until she sits
down at your table at lunch and asks you about your side of what
she's been hearing you tell her little and she says maybe you should
make a return visit to your birthplace in montana which came up in
conversation you go to the movies off campus just to get away from
the morass and run into the director of the mfa program heading
into a screening of the people vs larry flynt and the first
acknowledgment of the brouhaha comes when he says he's preparing
some remarks for graduation that'll be the final word on free speech
at bennington which he delivers to the confused crowd of parents
who have come hundreds and thousands of miles to see their own
graduate and know nothing of the controversy the president of the
college approaches you after the ceremony to assure you that she's

aware of the situation and that bennington will never tolerate censorship of any kind the student who burned your handout is kicked out of the program and you can feel people staring and pointing at you during the graduation dinner and after and the twinning of your narrative with ellis's is the only interesting residual thought you take away as you pass through the gates a graduate on your way to you don't know where oj simpson is forced to take the witness stand in the civil trial brought against him for the wrongful death of the murdered friend of his wife by the murdered friend's father who promises to haunt oj until the end of oj's days and oj brands his ex-wife a liar about all the domestic abuse she claimed to have suffered over the years at his hands his ex-wife unable to defend herself or tell her side of the story because she is dead bill cosby's son is murdered along the freeway in los angeles when he stops to help a stranded motorist the jury finds oj is probably liable for the deaths of his ex-wife and her friend and is ordered to pay tens of millions of dollars to the families of the murdered some employees of michael jackson's neverland ranch sue him for wrongful termination they claim was retribution for cooperating with the grand jury looking into allegations of child molestation by jackson word leaks the reclusive author j d salinger is going to publish a new book or at least a book-length revision of one of his old new yorker short stories a teacher in washington state is arrested for having sex with her twelve-year-old student she's pregnant with his child howard stern stars in the film version of his book private parts and is everywhere heavily promoting his story about growing up a kid listening to the radio to being on the radio and raising his profile via shock-jock antics the rapper biggie smalls is murdered in california after a party at an auto museum just like tupac shakur was killed in las vegas one car pulling up next to another and firing the murders are maybe related tit for tat three dozen or more people commit suicide together in an upscale house in san diego by drinking vodka laced with drugs and tying plastic bags around their heads in an effort to board a ufo they believed was trailing the hale-bopp comet you decide to make the move to new york city which means the end of your family living together in the same house your father and youngest brother taking an apartment and your younger brother moving in with friends your friends warn you that the thousand dollars you've saved for the move is hardly enough but you're impatient to go and the fact that you have a one-way ticket is an echo of the one-way ticket you had to alaska and though you were able to get home from that debacle you need the move to new york to be permanent returning the way you did from alaska will crush your spirits and leave you without options to live your life as you've dreamed the notion of the creative class burnished by your time at bennington you feel the pressure and the same night you land at your friend's apartment in queens you open your laptop and work on the novel you've started you like the symbolic gesture of moving to new york to write a novel based on the short story published by a new york literary magazine during the day you work on the novel but by midday you hop the n train into manhattan and waltz around famous landmarks like the empire state building the new york public library central park the plaza hotel poking your head into the oak bar imagining fitzgerald at the bar a gin in hand imagining the anecdote about him and zelda drunkenly splashing in the fountain out front you spend whole days walking up one side of manhattan and down the other riding the staten island ferry back and forth to see the statue of liberty you follow your friend's actor husband on errands to his agent's office to pick up scripts or to auditions waiting outside the apartment of the actor paul newman and his wife joanne woodward who are casting for a play you look up old friends from bennington who can't believe your talk about moving to new york wasn't just talk you visit one of your favorite faculty members susan cheever whose family you came to know at bennington you tag along with susan when she goes to pick up her son from school or join them on playdates the semblance of family welcome she invites you to her friend's house for coffee and the friend is a photographer who snaps a couple of pictures of you while you're not looking susan also invites you to a panel she's on at freds at barneys the posh restaurant in the basement of the famed department store on madison avenue the other panelists are the legendary newsman pete hamill and the actress isabella rossellini who you loved in blue velvet back in high school you can't stop gawking at the actress her skin so white it's translucent a few weeks into your move you realize in horror that your finances have dwindled to a couple hundred dollars well south of what will be required to secure an apartment of your own and a panic sets in about being deported back to arizona reprieve coming in the form of one of your bennington friends who lives in a farmhouse in concord just outside of boston offering up her basement apartment until you can figure out your next move you spend some of your last money on a bus ticket to boston promising yourself that the exile is only temporary the musician jeff buckley jumps into a river in memphis for a swim and his body washes up a week later a judge says mcdonald's needs to stop aiming its advertising at children another judge says the joe camel cigarette ads must be pulled for the same reason new york giants legend frank gifford is caught cheating on his wife with a flight attendant paid by a tabloid to do it the widow of malcolm x is burned by her grandson the person responsible for blowing up the truck in front of the federal building in oklahoma is found guilty and sentenced to death the boxer mike tyson bites off a piece of the ear of his opponent in a highly publicized boxing match and spits it onto the canvas stopping the fight concord is a wealthy hamlet that looks like a movie set the town center built around an ice cream shop a bookstore some restaurants and an old inn with history dating back to the american revolution you settle into the basement apartment and offer babysitting services for your friend's two small children in exchange for a quiet place to write the novel is coming along you think but the days are long and the summer days especially your friend lets you borrow her car to drive into the town center you notice a group of young people drinking at the bar at the colonial inn and fall in with them they're au pairs blowing off steam europeans working for the summer you're drawn to one in particular the belgian au pair and the summer quickly becomes not one of writing your way back to new york but of afternoon barbecues car trips to race point beach on cape cod a jazz festival in montreal you give in to the fact that you haven't had a girlfriend in half a decade and surrender to the welcome notion that someone likes you the way you've been liked before odds are long on you and the belgian au pair having a relationship not just because she's there only for the summer but because she has a boyfriend back home though without any prodding on your part you learn that the boyfriend back home is a long-expired relationship awaiting termination which encourages you but the boyfriend is also coming to america for a planned trip to hike the grand canyon of all places and as the date draws near you're surprised at how jealous you are even though all assurances are given by the belgian au pair robert mitchum dies from smoking and the next day jimmy stewart dies after he refuses to change the battery in his pacemaker the fashion designer gianni versace is murdered on the steps of his mansion in miami after running out for the morning paper the murderer identified as a serial killer on a spree from somewhere in the midwest for a week or so after everyone wonders where the serial killer is and then he's found hiding on a houseboat firing a bullet into his mouth as the police descend hundreds of virgins converge on the white house to celebrate abstinence the former receptionist at a little rock hotel who claims she was escorted by then governor bill clinton's bodyguard to clinton's hotel room and asked for sexual favors gets a trial date for her lawsuit against the president as the date of the belgian au pair's trip to the grand canyon with her boyfriend looms you find yourself in a state of despair then disbelief when your old friend the manager of the family print shop calls with the offer of flying you home to work for a week while he takes a family vacation cheaper and easier than hiring a temporary worker to take his place you agree immediately and the belgian au pair is apprehensive worried that you're engineering something but you swear you aren't though you can't believe your luck the belgian au pair and her boyfriend fly to phoenix ahead of you to take in the city you try not to think about it though you recommend some places worth seeing when you arrive you realize the boyfriend doesn't speak any english you volunteer to drive them to the grand canyon on the two-plus-hour trip north the boyfriend looks up every time you look in the rearview mirror he can't speak a lick of english but he clearly knows what's going on the belgian au pair is in dismay and you learn later that it ruined their trip which you swear to god was not your intention though you underestimated the tells of your body language and feel sorry for the verbal jabs and fights she had to endure while in the grand canyon back at the print shop for a week is old home week you've been gone for only three months and the fear that your attempt to move to new york is a farce drives you to fax your resume with your friend in concord's address and phone number to every literary agency in new york with a fax machine during lunch with your old friend the southern lawyer you lay out your adventures and the southern lawyer loans you three thousand dollars on the spot against whatever you sell your first book for to help get you back on your feet in new york city princess diana is killed when the car she's riding in crashes during a high-speed chase in paris to elude paparazzi as you leave phoenix for concord the governor who barely won election is convicted of extortion and bank fraud and resigns you and millions of others watch princess diana's funeral on television the two little princes walking along behind their mother's coffin it breaks your heart elton john's song about marilyn monroe that your younger brother loves becomes a song about the late princess only one literary agency calls about an interview in answer to your faxing but it's a famous one whose name you recognize you kiss the belgian au pair good-bye at the airport promising that you'll see each other again the first chance you get making tentative plans to reunite during the holidays on the bus ride back to new york city with the summer behind you and three thousand dollars minus a little in your bank account you interview at harold ober associates on madison avenue the clacking of typewriters greets you as you step through the door stenciled with the name of the firm perhaps as it was back when it was founded in 1929 your interview is with the president of the firm and you learn that the previous president a woman who worked directly for harold ober himself has just passed away you learn about the agency in full how most of its clients are long-dead famous writers like f scott fitzgerald sherwood anderson pearl s buck james m cain agatha christie william faulkner langston hughes joseph mitchell dylan thomas and of course j d salinger who isn't dead but just disappeared the interview takes place in the president's office under the low lighting of desk lamps and through a cloud of cigarette smoke which you guess must not be legal but everyone seems to be smoking and though you don't you don't mind you're offered the job but ask if you can start on september 24 not just because it's fitzgerald's birthday but because your old friend and fitzgerald fan from college who lives in princeton now wants to go on a pilgrimage to fitzgerald's grave in maryland your new boss is amused and all is agreed upon you take the train to princeton and the next morning you and your college friend light out for rockville maryland where the fitzgeralds are buried one on top of the other the closing words of the great gatsby etched in stone on a beveled flat marker where someone has left some cigarettes and an empty fifth of whiskey what you know about fitzgerald's funeral comes to you as sad a scene as gatsby's funeral a man who spent his life as an amusement to friends across two continents buried with few to no witnesses you can't believe the small catholic cemetery is surrounded by busy streets and commerce in the distance you can make out the sign for a furniture store and there's something plainly ignoble about the final resting place the end is the end is the end no matter who or where you wonder if fitzgerald ever daydreamed about his final resting place full of melancholy as he was you know he probably did and you wonder at the gulf between his imagination and reality though it hardly matters you and your friend grab a quick meal for the trip back to princeton eating on the trunk of her car in a shopping center designed by the grandfather of the actor edward norton whose family is from the area or so your friend thinks you take the train from princeton to new york just as fitzgerald did while he was in college so many of fitzgerald's observations about being on the outside looking in resonate and you think about him being from the midwest and you being from the west and now you ride the elevator to the tenth floor of the building on madison avenue just as fitzgerald did when he pushed through the same door you push every morning to start your day toiling in literary matters your job is little more than clerical sorting and distributing the afternoon mail answering the switchboard while the receptionist is at lunch transcribing your boss's daily dictation answering permissions requests to reprint material by ober clients the names and titles of books you love or at least have heard of adding a measure of intangible glamour to the position also a firsthand glimpse of the publishing game wrapping each manuscript as if it were your own anxious to hear back from the editor your boss sends it to disappointed if the manuscript is returned via courier with a declining letter exuberant when a book sells eager to let the author know all of it an inspiration to finish your novel you stay late after eating dinner at your desk so that you can work but also because you're camping out in the west village in the spare bedroom of a friend from bennington the former drummer for an indie rock band everyone loves and his artist wife and you don't want to be intrusive you've been pretending to be a student looking at the apartment postings on the board at the new school and other places but there's nothing you can afford and your friends are nice enough not to mind your residency in the spare room which has already been let to a high school kid who goes to school in vermont and comes to the city only sometimes his parents paying the rent so he'll have a place the kid tells you it's cool with him if you crash in his room and it seems like the perfect temporary housing the apartment is on the first floor above a twenty-four-hour deli on sixth avenue itself a carnival at all hours of the night you have to walk through the deli to the back to reach the stairs to the apartment sportscaster marv albert goes on trial for sodomizing and biting a women he'd known for years the tabloids full of details like a woman grabbing albert's toupee only for it to come off after four days of testimony albert pleads guilty to a lesser charge the promise keepers a christian organization for men founded by a former college football coach march on washington some suspect the group uses the bible to assert men's superiority over women especially in marriage a handful of women allegedly sexually harassed by president clinton are subpoenaed by the lawyers for paula jones after a month of looking you can't find an apartment share you can afford you're only making seven dollars an hour at harold ober but in truth it's a job you'd do for free and plus there's a line of people behind you figuratively who would love to have the job so you accept the invitation of a girl you know from bennington who lives with her husband and infant in a suburb of connecticut it takes two trains from grand central to reach the apartment but you have to agree and you don't mind the train ride though you smirk about being the only one without a briefcase or laptop but the worst part is the last train out of new york leaves at 10 pm so if you miss it you have to sleep at the office and if you miss the connecting train you have to pay for a cab to take you to the apartment the singer john denver is killed when the plane he is flying runs out of gas you go to see the writer denis johnson read from his new book at the new school and wonder if he remembers a time in the not-too-distant past when he visited the university of arizona and you asked him a couple of questions raising your hand when no one else would out of nervousness or whatever a girl you meet who works for george plimpton the legendary writer and founder of the literary magazine the paris review invites you to one of the equally legendary paris review parties at plimpton's house overlooking the east river the room filled with names and at least some faces you recognize from the literary world a famous television personality bumps you off the corner of the pool table doubling as a buffet table to get to the food you muster up the courage to approach plimpton and immediately invoke bret easton ellis's name and plimpton asks how bret is these days and looks at you as if you and only you can provide an update on bret's health and well-being and you shrug and say fine you say some complimentary things about the paris review and then beg off you feel like a fish swimming in the stream even if you're just a little fish the proximity of the big fish is reassuring inspiring you to keep moving on your novel which is almost finished you communicate by fax with the belgian au pair a fax always awaiting you in the morning because of the time difference phone calls are too expensive though the international faxes come out of your paycheck the longing on her end is palpable and you feel the same way and you promise to figure out a way to visit at thanksgiving though you have no idea if you can some friends from arizona visit and you take them to minetta tavern in the west village the dark-wood low-lit bar a block from the apartment of your friend the former drummer–turned–writer who introduced you to the place where you know the bar manager and his brother who is a waiter the bar has a long history the walls covered with drawings of the people who frequented the place all the way back to the 1800s when it was called the black rabbit some recent pictures too of brad pitt and other movie stars who have graced the booths the bar is busy for a sunday but starts to thin you and your friends inebriated thanks to the kind pour all night long the bar manager asks if you and your friends want to go to ac and you exhale loudly and shrug trying to buy time to figure out the code you've learned that half of everything in new york is pretending to be in the know even when you aren't your friends from arizona aren't shackled by the custom and ask what ac is and the bar manager announces that he's leaving in a limo with his brother the waiter for atlantic city and that you're welcome to join them you know you have to work the next day you know it's well after midnight already but your desire for the adventure with old friends overrides all rational thought and you pile into the white limousine when it appears the bar manager grabbing a bottle from behind the counter which you pass around as the limo leaves manhattan having never been to atlantic city you inquire as to how long the trip will take and are dismayed to learn that it's some two hours away your friends doze off and then you do too until you feel the contents of your stomach sloshing working their way back up your esophagus you ask about opening the moonroof for some air which you think might do the trick and you plunge your head through the opening a few minutes later a stream of cartoon vomit spraying from your mouth as the wind whips around you the sign for asbury park is the last thing you see before falling back into the limo and passing out when the limo pulls up under the casino portico the bar manager and his brother tell you to meet in a couple of hours if you want a ride back they're off to the high-stakes rooms you and your friends quickly lose some money on the slots ordering some free drinks that no one seems to want the sun is starting to rise it's after six with no sign of the limo or the bar manager if you leave right now you can still make it back to work you lean your head against the bus window your friends sleeping in seats across the aisle you sprint from the port authority on the west side of manhattan across fifth avenue to your job on madison avenue only to be excused by your boss who spying the vomit on your shirt asks if you're ill miracle of miracles you finish your novel based on the first short story you published and bret easton ellis agrees to read it and give you some feedback and you can't think about him actually reading your work without getting your hopes up the lead singer of the band inxs which you saw all those years ago in high school hangs himself in a hotel room maybe it's an accident maybe it's something else even a scurrilous rumor about autoerotic sex gone awry your inability to save any money lends credence to your suspicion that you'll be run out of new york by the end of the year unless you can sell your book for some decent money a good word from bret easton ellis would help but still you buy what you can't afford an airline ticket to belgium to visit the au pair somewhere in all the faxing you've become boyfriend and girlfriend she talks about selling the house her parents made her buy as an investment when she was young and moving to new york to study poetry which makes you nervous on a

number of levels you portray new york as a hard place to live which
it is though you suspect it's harder for some than others you haven't
spent enough time with the au pair to know which camp she's in you
pass through customs at the airport in brussels flashing the passport
you procured for the trip the transatlantic love affair feels like the
most romantic thing you've ever done though you're not sure what
the immediate future holds but you also try not to think about it the
airport reunion is joyous and you both laugh about how it's been
only twelve weeks since you've seen each other but it feels like
forever the summer in concord a memory the personalities already
ghosts in your memories even though you're exhausted on the drive
to antwerp you're too wired to rest hungry too you stop at a small
outbuilding just outside antwerp and you both point at rolled meats
under fluorescent lights that are quickly dropped into a deep-fat
fryer you both happily munch at the kitchen table of her one-
bedroom house drinking beer which she reminds you has a higher
alcohol content than american beer you're just two lovers playing
house making plans for the next couple of days which include
meeting her parents for dinner at their house you do a little laundry
before the short trip to her parents' but stuff too many clothes into
the dryer so that your nice black shirt isn't dry not even close when
it's time to leave so you put it on wet hoping no one will notice her
father a small but sturdy man looks you in the eye as he grips your
hand pumping it casually you've been warned that her father is stern
which immediately puts you in mind to win him over her mother
smiles nervously as you are introduced her sisters less nervous than
curious you take the chair set out for you in the living room and they
gather around to ask you questions the au pair translating back and
forth though everyone seems to understand english everyone sits
down to chinese food and you tell the story about your wet shirt and
soon you are offered a warm sweatshirt also offered glass after glass
of wine her father leaving the table and returning with another
bottle more than once you are twice the size of anyone in the room
and are sure you can hold your liquor so when you wake the next

morning back at the au pair's house it is a surprise that at some point you slumped over at the table much to her father's amusement you're assured her father likes you and that is really all you were going for why do you sleep on couches she asks disdain in her voice you can't find the words to express how much you love new york how it feels like home to you even though you have no home to call your own it makes no sense to her and you get into a small skirmish when you decline her offer to move in with her you can't imagine what you'd do all day but she offers that you can write which sounds ideal but something instinctively tells you it's not the answer but she feels like you've made a choice between her and something else no one can put a name to when you part at the brussels airport you promise to come back in a few weeks at christmas hoping that you'll receive a christmas bonus large enough to cover the trip the actor chris farley is found dead in his chicago apartment from a drug overdose paula jones's lawyers subpoena a former white house intern in jones's ongoing sexual harassment suit against the president the director woody allen marries the adopted daughter of his former lover the actress mia farrow who played daisy in the film version of the great gatsby when you pack for the trip back to belgium at christmas you let your friend in connecticut know you won't return and you're not sure if that means just to her apartment or if it means something more you're welcomed like a long-lost son-in-law by the au pair's family when you return but outside of a nice christmas dinner at their house you don't see them your old high school friend from phoenix flies to london and you and the au pair meet him there for a planned trip to celebrate hogmanay the new year's celebration in edinburgh you and your high school friend have always talked about attending but first you stop north of london at the house of a girl your friend met in his travels abroad the house is in willoughby waterleys a small village with a pub at the end of the lane the girl's house is a two-story georgian called the old rectory and she's there with her mother and sisters her youngish father having recently and tragically died while working in the garden the house cast in a pall but in english fashion you're received and put up in the part of the house that has heat you're asked to sign the guest book and you notice the actress helena bonham carter has recently signed it too the next day is spent mostly in the pub followed by a lively dinner with the girl and her family conversation ranges from american politics to european art and you have fun playing the cosmopolitan delivering one-liners and laughing at zingers the au pair excuses herself from the table and after she's gone for an uncomfortably long time you offer a meager joke about her having gotten lost and go after her you find her in your room packing her bag what are you doing are you sick you ask i don't know you she says hatefully concentrating on her packing you ask what she means and she says listening to you at the table she had no idea who was talking about all these things you were talking about where do they come from she demands to know you do your best to calm her down you say you have no idea what she means but intuitively you know you've been speaking to her in clipped sentences and simple thoughts which started as a shorthand but has become how you communicate you snatch her passport now you can't leave you say playing for laughter i'm leaving she says emphatically you get her to agree to sit for ten minutes in silence with you and if she still wants to leave you'll help her figure out how and after ten minutes she announces that she's going to bed in the morning you and the au pair and your high school friend light out for the house in crawford-upon-john another village with a pub but this time in scotland where your high school friend has rented a house for hogmanay assuring you that you're welcome to stay too the housemates are of various nationalities german swedish dutch and they greet you and the au pair warmly a trip to glasgow planned for the following day is scuttled by the ferocious winds that rock the house imprisoning everyone trapped everyone resigns themselves to a day of board games and drinking you sniff some commentary from the other dutchman in the house that the part of belgium the au pair comes from is considered backward and uncosmopolitan comparatively you ignore the taunts

exuberant after a restless night to finally be on your way to edinburgh
desperate to escape the glumness pervading the house   the
atmosphere in edinburgh is festive and as the day expires the city
center swells with eager faces you and the au pair set up camp in the
window of a pub on the royal mile and begin drinking in earnest
your high school friend wants to float down the river of people but
the au pair is happy where she is you promise not to be gone long as
you're swept up in the momentum of the human parade you
somehow swim back to the au pair before midnight when auld lang
syne issues forth the hogmanay tradition of kissing everyone around
you for the duration of the song commences and the au pair is
besieged with kisses before you step in for your own private
celebration your high school friend kisses his way down the royal
mile and has a nasty cold sore in the morning as proof saying good-
bye to the au pair at heathrow you truly have no idea when you'll see
her again the novelty of the transatlantic romance seems to have
worn off for both of you and now real decisions must be made one
of robert kennedy's sons dies when he hits a tree while skiing in
aspen your friend the former drummer–turned–writer and his wife
the artist with the apartment in the west village once again rescue
you by letting you stay in their spare bedroom and you promise
them it's only temporary that you're going to find some kind of
permanent living situation you're surprised when bret easton ellis
returns the copy of the manuscript you gave him and it's covered
with edits in black ink you can't believe he read the novel so closely
and you set about spending all your free time in the conference
room at harold ober working on the edits one night one of the agents
spies you working and asks what you're working on and she says to
let her read it when you're finished sonny from sonny and cher dies
when he hits a tree while skiing in nevada the teacher in washington
state impregnated by her twelve-year-old student is released from
prison early and told to stay away from the student monica lewinsky
files an affidavit in the paula jones lawsuit denying she had a sexual
relationship with president clinton and a week or so later president

clinton gives similar testimony in addition to the helpful line editing on your novel bret easton ellis has suggested some wholesale changes to the structure which you accept without question someone named matt drudge runs an e-mail newsletter about politics and hollywood gossip and he includes an item about a story by a newsweek magazine reporter about some secretly taped conversations that monica lewinsky's colleague at the pentagon recorded where lewinsky admits having sexual relations with the president drudge's story is just about how the newsweek story was suppressed internally but a couple of days later the scandal hits all the press outlets at once it seems bret easton ellis even suggests some lines to add here and there and you add them all a group of texas cattle ranchers sue oprah winfrey over a show she did a couple of years earlier about beef production in the era of mad cow disease the cattle ranchers claim the show cost them tens of millions in lost beef sales you write a letter to charles scribner on ober letterhead asking if you can meet with him to discuss the scribner history as it relates to harold ober you're thinking about compiling a history of harold ober and he agrees the old scribner building is a block away but is also a clothing store now but scribner's current offices are in the neighborhood and you keep the appointment the third-generation charles scribner is affable and lively as he regales you with some clearly well-worn chestnuts about the golden days of publishing but you do learn something you were ignorant of before the fact that fitzgerald dealt directly with scribner on the contracts for his books using harold ober only for the sale of his short stories because there was so much money in short story sales and very little in the sale of books you're incredulous but when you check the ober files for the contract for the great gatsby you see it's true president clinton reiterates his denials about a sexual relationship with his former intern the only question the press wants to ask him your boss helps you arrange a phone conversation with harold ober's son to learn a little more about his father who is described as a blue-blood yankee from harvard and you both chuckle about what he must've thought of

fitzgerald that ober was exactly the type of person fitzgerald was
envious of his whole life the son encourages your nascent project
and asks you to keep him posted which you promise to do the last
living ober client who knew fitzgerald personally lives in concord
your old stomping grounds and you write a letter asking to interview
the writer the letter is answered by his daughter who tells you the
writer is ill but is looking forward to talking to you on the train to
boston you admit what you've been denying about the au pair that
the relationship has probably petered out the international faxes
becoming less frequent though she still professes to love you but
your concern is that the more time you spend together the more ill-
suited you seem and how can anything be known with so many
miles between you your bennington friend picks you up from the
train station and you realize how nice it is to get out of the concrete
city and into the green suburbs if only briefly you call to confirm
your arrival the next day for the interview and the writer's daughter
tells you the writer passed away the previous weekend and that the
writer thought you were supposed to come the previous weekend
the unspoken idea being that he'd been holding on long enough to
talk to you but when you didn't show that was that the daughter is
distracted by her grief and doesn't hear your apologies the teacher in
washington state on parole for having sex with her twelve-year-old
student is arrested again when the two are found having sex in her
car where she becomes pregnant again monica lewinsky postpones
the deposition she was to give in the paula jones case now that the
whole world is watching you turn in the finished version of your
novel to the agent who asked and she reads it over the weekend
professing her love for it and the following week she begins
submitting it to publishers you can't believe you have a manuscript
being read by editors in new york city but you have to keep a brave
face when the first editor the agent queries turns the book down
there are plenty of other editors you're assured and so the long
process of trying to find a match with an editor begins monica
lewinsky wants immunity from kenneth starr who is leading the

investigation of president clinton and his alleged misdeeds a white male in his thirties is arrested at sky harbor airport in phoenix for verbally abusing an airport employee and it turns out to be axl rose the front man of guns n' roses that no one has seen in years the rumor is he lives in a mansion by the ocean in california and never leaves it just rehearsing and rehearsing music no one will ever hear the au pair surprises you by showing up unannounced in new york for valentine's day since you're just crashing in your friend's extra room you scramble to pay for a hotel with money you can't really afford to waste which sets the tone for her visit you refusing to move to belgium her refusing to believe that you don't want to or at least wouldn't benefit from the stability you can't find the words to explain to her that your life in new york is just beginning or so it seems but also it feels selfish to admit that you're more invested in that narrative than the one that began the summer before and a few days after she returns home you say into the phone that it's best if you both call it off she refuses to agree telling you that you'll have to hang up on her because she's not going to agree and you beg her not to make you but she repeats herself and you replace the phone in its cradle and wipe your slick cheeks before returning to work president clinton argues that paula jones's lawsuit should be thrown out or at least delayed until he's no longer president more editors send polite rejection letters for your novel but you continue to hope for the best knowing it could take a year or more for the agent to work her way through all the publishers big and small a homemade sex tape of the actress pamela anderson and her husband tommy lee the drummer for the heavy-metal band mötley crüe stolen by a disgruntled electrician working on their house becomes available to the public for purchase the actress and the drummer claim the tape has been leaked widely enough that the only recourse is to strike a distribution deal to receive a share of the monies for the video you saw it when it first came out at a brunch thrown by the music video editor for atlantic records you met through your former drummer–turned–writer friend the video lives up to the hype but you can't decide if tommy

and pamela are truly that exhibitionist or if they knew in their heart
of hearts that others might one day see the video an editor declines
to publish your novel saying if he were still working at the previous
house where he'd worked he'd publish it in a second which seems
like a compliment but doesn't sit like one kenneth starr subpoenas
the bookstore where monica lewinsky shops and learns that she
recently purchased a copy of vox by nicholson baker a book in the
form of a phone sex conversation the agent representing you comes
to your desk and says she shouldn't tell you this but she just got off
the phone with an editor who is halfway through your book and
knows he wants to buy it the publisher is one of the smaller ones so
the money wouldn't be spectacular but the publisher is well regarded
which could mean some critical success you have a hard time
refraining from mentioning this bit of intel to your friends who are
curious how it's going the judge throws out paula jones's sexual
harassment suit against president clinton one half of the disgraced
musical duo milli vanilli the ones who had to give back their grammy
when it was revealed they were lip-synchers is found dead in his
hotel room from a drug overdose on the eve of the release of milli
vanilli's comeback album featuring actual vocals from the duo
there's no word from the editor who wants to publish your book but
the agent says to give him a little more time a show from britain
called teletubbies debuts on pbs and everyone gaggles about how
weird the teletubbies are wondering what exactly they're supposed
to be and why they have televisions for stomachs the anxiety about
the silence from the editor interested in publishing your novel is
distracting and your agent finally places a call to see if there's any
news and she looks ashen when she reports that the editor left
suddenly to go work for aol his office having already been cleaned
out you're devastated but relieved that you never mentioned a word
of it to anyone and you put all your hopes on the editors who are still
considering the book a man follows the pop singer george michael
into a bathroom at will rogers park in beverly hills and says show me
yours and i'll show you mine and when he does the man who is a

cop arrests him for engaging in a lewd act drinks with friends at minetta's for your birthday and you're standing at the crowded bar trying to get the bar manager's attention and when you look in the mirror behind the bar you see the actor who played ferris bueller is standing next to you and it takes everything you have not to turn to him and tell him how much you loved ferris and fancied that you were him when you were in high school and when you wake in the morning with a concussive headache you're proud of yourself for having not said a word president clinton holds his first public press conference since the lewinsky scandal broke and is livid about the inquiry initiated by kenneth starr frank sinatra dies and the empire state building is lit up blue as a tribute you stumble to the subway after a night of drinking and all the bars are blasting sinatra music your colleague at harold ober the other assistant has been asking if you want to hang out he's a lot younger than you are just like all the assistants in publishing and so you put it off but then one night agree and end up shooting pool with him and his friend who is an assistant to one of the editors who read your novel the friend really liked the novel and says so which means more to you than it should the comedian phil hartman is murdered in his sleep by his wife while their two children sleep in their rooms in the same house the wife flees and brings back a friend to try to help her figure out what to do and when the friend isn't looking she locks herself in the house and commits suicide a friend who runs the print shop at memorial sloan kettering cancer center scores two tickets to the yankees game which stops with a rain delay you don't know anything about baseball but know the history of yankee stadium however the awe wears off the more it rains and the drunker everyone gets the game finally restarts and the opposing team the hated rival boston red sox score right away and your friend being from boston cheers them on to the dismay of those around you and some guys want to make an issue of it but your friend won't back down and you sit tense wondering what will happen next but then the yankees start winning which is the balm the situation needs you're starting to become a regular at george plimpton's place on east seventy-second street this time for a book party for a novelist who dedicated his book to bret easton ellis which is your only interest in attending save for the free food and drinks you meet the writer jonathan ames who is in awe of plimpton and fitzgerald and seems to emulate both not just fitzgerald's sensitivity but also the tenets of plimpton's participatory journalism plimpton having written about the time he quarterbacked for the detroit lions or pitched to willie mays or took a bullet from john wayne you recall fitzgerald's advice to his daughter when she professed wanting to become a writer you can't do something for the sake of writing about it but george plimpton surely could and did the writer at bennington who helped save you from the debacle of the teacher who disappeared is reading at the national arts club a private club that once boasted mark twain as a member you're concerned about the dress code when you see a sign that gentlemen must wear jackets after 5 pm but the only true hassle is the bartender who refuses to see you your boss at harold ober agrees to let you train to princeton on fridays to root around in the ober archives for your history of harold ober project you stroll the princeton quad passing students roughly your age wondering if they mistake you for one of their own you stand before the house on prospect avenue where fitzgerald lived as a student hunting fitzgerald's ghost in every corner of campus the irony of his being one of princeton's most famous alums even though he never actually graduated you finally settle into a chair in firestone library and summon the first box of the ober archives gingerly flipping through files of yellowed typewritten letters surprising in their lack of detail about ober the man letters devoid of gossip or news of the day your hope of preserving a romantic history fluttering away as you comb through the boxes and you end up canceling the weekly train trips a few weeks into the project one of the spice girls ginger spice announces that she's leaving the all-girl supergroup in order to launch a solo career a respite in the cobbling together of beds and couches comes in the form of a room to rent inside a warehouse in an industrial section of brooklyn called dumbo an unfortunate acronym for down under the manhattan bridge overpass dumbo is little more than artists squatting in their studios there are no services and at night the streets become deadly quiet but the room is cheap and so you move your stuff into a building with a helmet factory on the fifth floor the window in your small room overlooks the power plant next door the east river just beyond and you think about how just up the river is george plimpton's opulent apartment and how that's worlds away from where you'll be resting your head your roommate is an artist friend of the artist going out with the former drummer– turned–writer which is how you heard of the sublet your roommate's art is across many mediums but one of the more recent ones is her painting her body in latex and then performing at local burlesque shows stripping down and then stripping her skin you see one of these performances on a videotape you mistake for a movie one day when you're home sick from work president clinton is subpoenaed in the lewinsky matter a few days later lewinsky meets with kenneth starr and admits to a sexual encounter with the president the very next day lewinsky is granted immunity president clinton agrees to testify voluntarily lewinsky hands over one of her dresses which rumor has it contains some of the president's dna on it the little kid from diff'rent strokes everyone loved is arrested for punching a woman who asks for his autograph while he's shopping for a bulletproof vest for his job as a security guard paula jones's lawyers appeal to have her lawsuit against the president reinstated bret easton ellis invites you to dinner at the bowery bar a chic bar and grill a known haunt of actors and models bret also invites two other writers he knows one of them you know as a writer whose work bret discovered as a zine in tower records bret recommended the writer to someone and the writer got a book deal so you're naturally a little jealous but you honestly think the writer's work isn't very good but maybe that's just jealousy the other writer is someone bret attended bennington with and you're starting to feel like a fish out of water until bret favorably mentions your as-yet-unpublished novel to the others and they pepper you with sincere questions about it and wish you good luck trying to get it published and you admit that you suspect it's not going to happen they suggest starting something new and whether or not you will feels like a test of your confidence in your first novel finding a publisher immunity in hand monica lewinsky testifies before the grand jury you relax on the porch of the davis alumni house at bennington college taking in the summer landscape as you and your friend from boston await the arrival of your fellow benningtonites the former drummer–turned–writer and his artist girlfriend as well as the woman who lent you her basement apartment in concord the five of you chipping in to rent the house to get some work done faced with the reality that your first novel has been seen by every publisher in and out of new york without garnering any interest you know you need to start a new writing project the consistent criticism about your first novel being too dark stung even though books that are dark or called small are considered literary the preferred label of most writers you know your time as a student at bennington impressed upon you that literary distinction is preferable to money or wide readership a theory that your job in publishing has all but erased you wonder if it isn't possible to shoot for both and you have this in mind when you spend your week at the alumni house casting about for ideas for a new book lighting on the notion of using your second published story we're so famous as a springboard for a novel the short story is only eight pages long so there's room to enlarge the narrative around the theme of celebrity obsession you're thinking about a gentle criticism of society's infatuation with frivolity and minutiae about celebrities nothing overt or harsh especially since you're in no way above the fray though part of you feels manipulated into being interested in things you wouldn't normally care about you use the first-person voice of the short story and just start writing and by the end of the week you have close to eighty pages having taken breaks only for dinner and nightly carousing with the others you're so excited about the new pages that you show them to your agent back at ober hoping she'll be excited too but she frowns and complains that the book makes women look dumb you're so upset that you put the pages in a drawer and try to forget them instead researching small foreign publishers who might be interested in publishing your first novel outside of america which you're fine with president clinton becomes the first sitting president to give testimony to a grand jury investigating him he goes on television after giving his testimony and admits that he had an improper relationship with monica lewinsky but did not have sexual relations with her there's a rumor in the press that the president has submitted a dna sample to kenneth starr and word about monica lewinsky's unlaundered blue dress leaks out major league baseball players mark mcgwire and sammy sosa are in a race to break the long-held single-season home run record and mcgwire finally does in a game against sosa's team kenneth starr turns in the results of his investigation and calls for the impeachment of president clinton whose four-hour grand jury testimony is leaked to the networks who air it in full bret easton ellis calls you at work to tell you that you're mentioned in a new york times article about kgb bar where you and your former drummer–turned–writer friend will be reading your short stories published in literary magazines you run across the street and buy a copy showing everyone in the office the full-page article staring at your name in print the woman who previously stalked late-night host david letterman stealing his porsche and sleeping near the tennis courts of his home in connecticut kneels in front of a train in colorado the house of representatives authorizes an impeachment inquiry against president clinton sportscaster marv albert's criminal record is wiped clean after a year of good behavior two teens in wyoming pretend to be gay and lure an openly gay kid to a remote area and beat and rob him and chain him to a fence where he's discovered eighteen hours after he dies less than a week later from his beating president clinton signs legislation meant to prepare the government for the upcoming millennium-bug problem something about banks not being able to recognize the year 2000 because they previously used only two digits instead of four when writing computer software not just banks but lots of problems maybe on the horizon some say it'll be the end of civilization when computers think the year 2000 is really the year 1900 the actor michael j fox who played that kid you loved on that show when you were a kid and all the back to the future movies too announces he has parkinson's disease the new york tabloids are ablaze with headlines about the comedian jerry seinfeld and a woman he met at a health club who was recently married to the son of a prominent theater family the woman ends the marriage after four months and begins dating seinfeld president clinton settles with paula jones over her lawsuit without admitting any wrongdoing among your cherished responsibilities working at harold ober is opening the mail as a kid you would join fan clubs and send away for things just to have a reason to run to the mailbox at ober the mail arrives in two or three mailbags every afternoon and it's your job to sort the query letters manuscripts royalty statements fan mail and the like the most interesting mail is always from j d salinger bearing a typewritten return address somewhere in vermont the envelopes usually stuffed with items salinger considers a nuisance or matters he needs his agent your boss to handle directly the cover letter to his agent your boss is never signed though salinger prints his name anything with his signature is considered valuable and owing to some contracts recently stolen from the agency that handles his foreign rights you spend a couple of days photocopying all of ober's correspondence and contracts involving salinger and shredding the originals under the eye of your boss there is something admirable in the way salinger refuses any of his work to be reprinted or adapted the television show freaks and geeks writes for permission to use a copy of the catcher in the rye as a prop in a scene and ober responds with salinger's long-standing policy against such a thing hoping the producers wouldn't ferret out that when the mel gibson julia roberts movie conspiracy theory asked to use the book as a central prop to the movie and were told no they realized they didn't need permission a start-up called amazon sends over a script for a proposed television

commercial featuring delivery of a box to a house in the woods
wherein the house's occupant merely slats the blinds as the delivery
person walks past a mailbox emblazoned with the name salinger
which ober declines even though you all laugh about it around the
office but any whiff of infringement is no laughing matter the fbi
has been involved in a case going back to the 1970s when someone
offered for sale a book of all twenty-two of salinger's short stories
selling them all over the country out of the back of a vehicle no one
could describe by a bookseller that no one could identify the
burgeoning internet provides an avenue for further sales of the
bootleg book and when ober notices it for sale on the auction site
ebay we write them a letter demanding they remove the item ebay's
initial response is the standard fare that outside of body parts and
other egregiousness they are not responsible for the content of
auctions transacted on their site but a second letter warning them of
their complicity in trafficking in copyright infringement brings the
desired result and you are assigned a new daily routine perusing
ebay for illegal salingeralia the question you field the most from
friends is whether or not the catcher in the rye will ever be made
into a movie and you say not in the author's lifetime it's his wish for
all his work that none of it be adapted for film some story about a
disaster the time one of his short stories was filmed with his
permission so when an advance article appears in the new york
times about an iranian film festival at lincoln center that will feature
a film based on salinger's franny and zooey the ober forces mobilize
quickly the attorney ober keeps on retainer on salinger's behalf is
apprised of the situation and though there's no copyright convention
between the united states and iran preventing the making of the
film the fact that the film is being shown on united states soil will
make it easy to quash on the grounds that it is a violation of salinger's
copyright your boss lays this out in a letter to salinger with the note
asking for further instructions from him the timing is bad though
as your boss is leaving on one of the scarce vacations she takes so in
her letter to salinger she tells him just to call and talk to you about

what he wants to do your boss tells you that the author is suffering from some deafness and that you'll have to shout into the phone if he calls you don't think he'll really call so you're surprised when you pick up the phone at your desk and the deep gravelly voice on the other end says your name with a question mark at the end in an accusatory way and then says salinger here i think we ought to do something about this thing you tell him you'll give the message to the lawyer and salinger says very good and then good-bye when you hang up you are a little shaken by what has just transpired the same as if you'd seen a ghost the lawyer stops the showing at lincoln center and the whole matter disappears just like that your friend from bennington who lives in brooklyn has been working on a memoir about drinking in bars every night and to celebrate the near end he invites everyone he knows to mcsorley's old ale house where he'll be in residence for twelve straight hours you go for a lot of it happy to celebrate the success of his fieldwork but also the end of another year in new york for you with all its ups and downs bret easton ellis invites you to his annual christmas party one of the more exclusive holiday parties and you make the mistake of attending alone thinking that you aren't allowed to bring anyone but when you arrive you see that bret's loft has been cleared of all furniture save for a stereo system in the corner screeching at levels making conversation intolerable bret shyly hiding in the corner near the stereo console while people approach him you also bring a christmas gift a photocopy of the contract for the great gatsby but no one else has brought anything and you submarine the manila envelope near the catered food and get in line for a drink nodding at bret who maybe does or doesn't see you recognize some faces but not the girl who is standing next to you hanging on the extremely tall guy you recognize as one of the editors behind the new york literary magazine open city but then the girl turns in profile and you see it's the actress parker posey and you just smile and nod rather than make a fuss about how great you think she is the population of the loft doubles and triples it seems and you think there's no way all these people were invited and without finishing your drink you escape grabbing your coat from the coat check bret has set up in the lobby of his building president clinton is impeached by the house of representatives for lying under oath and obstructing justice only the second president in history to be impeached after andrew johnson who was impeached for removing the secretary of war and replacing him with ulysses s grant the new year opens with clinton's senate trial by now the facts and alleged facts of the matter well known basketball player michael jordan retires for the last time and for good you head up to bennington with some friends to hang around the residency see old teachers and participate on a publishing panel extolling what you've gleaned about working in publishing without trying to sound too defeatist you don't let the reality that you're an alum with a novel that failed to sell ruin the homecoming back in new york you see the writer jonathan ames in his one-man show oedipussy and witness firsthand how much ames idolizes george plimpton the show an incredible bridge between ames's work and his persona you think about how having a persona is oftentimes the difference between the mortal and immortal especially when it comes to writers there's always some memorable backstory stories outside the covers of their books that keep authors alive in everyone's imagination none more than fitzgerald but also bret easton ellis whom you have drinks with the following night bret amused by all you tell him about jonathan's show you also let him know that your first novel failed to find a publisher and he encourages you just to move on from it and you remember the pages of the new project you shelved and look them over devising a way to revise the material so that the entire novel isn't told from just one point of view which you suspect is what turned your agent off the televangelist jerry falwell warns parents that one of the teletubbies the one called tinky winky is really gay and bad for children a twenty-two-year-old immigrant from guinea is shot forty-one times on the landing of his apartment in the bronx by four police officers who mistake him for a rape suspect and further mistake his reaching for his wallet as him reaching for a gun you place another short story with a small literary magazine which gives you some much-needed confidence as you dive into the revision of we're so famous the senate votes to acquit president clinton of his impeachment charges the thing over except for everyone's divided opinions about it you pitch the idea of editing an all-interview issue of the mississippi review using your interview with bret easton ellis as a centerpiece and are awarded the commission you tap your closest bennington friends to come on board and interview their favorite writers everyone excited about the project the film critic gene siskel who owns the suit john travolta wore in the movie saturday night fever dies from complications after surgery for brain cancer your friend from college your former literary magazine coeditor blows through new york with her best friend who happens to work for notorious boxing promoter don king and who can get tickets to practically anything and invites you to the broadway show cabaret featuring the actress jennifer jason leigh attending the show you realize there are whole swaths of new york you know nothing about the broadway district one of them that cabaret is based on the writings of christopher isherwood a writer you're vaguely familiar with comes as a surprise you've previously given no thought to the idea of musicals being based on literary works doctor jack kevorkian the euthanasia booster present at a number of suicides over the years is arrested when he actually helps someone commit suicide the magician david blaine is buried in a plastic coffin under a tank of water for a week across the street from trump plaza everyone stopping by to have their picture taken with the entombed magician you move out of the warehouse in dumbo and back into the spare bedroom in the west village apartment of your friend the former drummer–turned–writer and his artist girlfriend the rapper puff daddy is arrested for assaulting the manager of another rapper over a crucifixion scene in a music video you and your friend the former drummer–turned–writer are asked to teach a hemingway story to a class of high school students at the kennedy library in boston for the hemingway centennial the hemingway room at the kennedy library is a memorial to the writer and his life and works you're not much of a hemingway fan having long ago chosen fitzgerald's side of the literary contretemps promoted through legend though you recognize that the idea of having to choose sides is ridiculous same as the east coast/west coast rap thing two seniors dressed in trench coats walk into their colorado high school and open fire killing twelve students and a teacher and injuring almost two dozen other students before committing suicide in the school's library the all-interview issue of the mississippi review comes together easily and you turn everything in eager to see it in print on the eve of being retried by the government your old boss charles h keating jr pleads guilty to wire and bankruptcy fraud and receives a sentence of time already served ending the legal proceedings against him you sell another short story to a literary magazine a little bit of a roll happening the girl who played the sister on diff'rent strokes dies of an accidental overdose love letters between j d salinger and a college girl he famously seduced are sold by the college girl at auction at sotheby's and purchased by a software magnate who returns them to salinger via harold ober and you shred them while your boss watches you turn in the final draft of your new novel we're so famous to your agent but she still doesn't like it well enough to represent it but you beg her to try a few publishers just to see agreeing to drop the matter if the editors concur the agent agrees sportscaster marv albert is given back his old job at nbc bret easton ellis invites you to drinks with jay mcinerney at a bar called pop around the corner from bret's loft in the east village and mcinerney makes a crack about bret traveling a long distance and you watch in amusement as they banter back and forth the handful of editors your agent sends we're so famous to decline the manuscript and that's that though you still feel strongly about the book you send it on your own to your colleague's friend the one you shot pool with and who said he liked your first book but the manuscript comes back your colleague's friend having left his job the small plane piloted by john f kennedy jr goes missing on a flight from new jersey to his family's compound on martha's vineyard where he was to attend the wedding of a cousin president clinton orders u.s. navy warships to assist in the search and the wreckage and bodies of kennedy and his wife and the wife's sister are found five days later you take the subway down to the loft apartment in tribeca where jfk jr lived to see the shrine of flowers and photos and notes no one can figure out for sure if the movie the blair witch project is real or not you see it even though you don't really like horror films and you can't tell but think the marketing campaign is to blame for the confusion which is the filmmaker's intention and everyone proclaims the use of the internet in this way as genius the government pays the heirs of abraham zapruder tens of millions of dollars rather than relinquish the footage of kennedy's assassination they confiscated that november day in dallas a couple you don't know personally but who are friends of friends abandon their apartment in queens for a better apartment the rent all paid up on the old place so you buy an inflatable mattress and camping lantern and sleep on the floor of the empty apartment the early-morning light streaming in through the curtainless rooms when the month is over you're able to crash temporarily on the couch in the upper east side apartment of your agent who spends most of her time upstate the literary agent's boyfriend a bartender and the father of the actor dylan mcdermott is your roommate though you hardly see each other the calendar turns to october and you're out of couches and connections to places to sleep so you move your meager possessions into the harold ober offices the hardest part about living at ober is fooling the twenty-four-hour doormen whom you simply befriend rather than insult they look the other way when you sneak a bag of laundry out of the building or when you duck out early in the morning to grab a shower at the health club you join on a trial membership for just that purpose you sleep on your boss's floor because of the padding under her rug which is the most comfortable spot a dancer you meet through your bennington friend writing the bar memoir is called away on tour and you sublet her tiny studio apartment in brooklyn while she's away michael jackson's wife debbie rowe files for divorce a new show on television that claims to be unscripted debuts apparently people are stuck in the wild and have to participate in rounds of challenges to earn points for the right to stay the learjet carrying golfer payne stewart from florida to texas veers off course and the fighters that scrambled to escort it see that everyone inside is dead they follow the jet north and rather than shoot it down they wait for it to run out of fuel which it does and crashes in a field in south dakota you track down your colleague's friend who liked your first novel who is now working at a different publisher and send him we're so famous the mississippi review selects a short story you wrote for inclusion in their prize issue when the dancer returns you're homeless again and your agent lets you stay at her place again as she'll be away for most of november and december for the holidays after some serious deliberations your friend the former drummer–turned–writer and you decide to join the movement of literary magazines being founded in new york by starting your own you use what contacts you have to learn about distribution subscription drives how to keep databases and how to avoid production nightmares you both assemble a staff made up of friends from bennington and from your travels in new york one of the fiction editors suggests calling the magazine post road since half the editors are in new york and half are in boston and all the founding editors are excited for the venture the rapper jay z is arrested for stabbing a record executive your boss throws a christmas party at her apartment and you meet ira levin the longtime harold ober client who wrote rosemary's baby and other famous books you shower him with praise even though you haven't read his work a practice that has now become rote but levin's humility strikes you and you engage him in a conversation about the history of harold ober of which he says he's proud to be a part the beatle george harrison is stabbed in his home by an intruder the rapper puff daddy and his girlfriend the actress jennifer lopez are at a new york city nightclub where a scuffle breaks out shots are fired and the rapper is arrested as the clock counts down to the year 2000 the overzealous wait with bated breath for the end of times but when the calendar turns to january all that really happens is a couple of credit card machines refuse to process sales and a bank of slot machines at a casino in delaware all quit working a friend of a friend knows someone in williamsburg brooklyn where your friend who is writing the bar memoir lives who needs a roommate and you move in your room is fully furnished with the stuff from the previous tenant the best friend of your new roommate but best friend no more as he started sleeping with his friend's girlfriend who was also living in the apartment the friend and the girlfriend having decamped the common bathroom has no lights so you buy some battery-powered lighting for use in the middle of the night you've all but given up on hearing from your colleague's friend and the new year brings the sober reality that you're starting from square one writing-wise but then an e-mail arrives in your inbox from your colleague's friend in his capacity at bloomsbury usa the american publishing arm of the british publisher that has made piles of dough publishing the harry potter books asking if you'd be interested in having your novel published as a paperback original meaning it wouldn't come out as a hardcover and meaning that there wouldn't be a lot of review coverage since paperback originals are hardly reviewed but you hardly care about that and you say yes definitely and your colleague's friend answers that in that case he'd like to acquire the book and publish it your new editor writes back with effusive praise for the novel and says he'll get an official offer to you in a day or two having seen publishing deals at ober fall apart you keep the great news of your impending publication to yourself also genuinely afraid of jinxing the prospect an idea you think ridiculous until your editor seems to disappear two days three days a week goes by with no word you don't want to start your publishing relationship off panicking about the offer so you busy yourself at work glad that you didn't say anything to anyone about the e-mail the colleague you have in common with your new editor has long since left ober and so you have no insight into what's going on you think about whether or not the book deal is real every second of every minute of the day the rapper puff daddy is charged in the incident in the nightclub with jennifer lopez all of the post road editors begin soliciting work for their respective sections fiction poetry nonfiction theater criticism and art the band rage against the machine plays a concert on wall street and the swelling crowds cause the markets to close early for security reasons you look up from your desk to find the film agent and the foreign-rights agent two colleagues that have like everyone at ober come to seem like family the agents smile and hand you the fax from bloomsbury usa with the offer for we're so famous word leaks out quickly and everyone congratulates you your new editor e-mails to say he's faxed the offer apologizing for the delay but he was out for two weeks with the flu offer in hand you tell your friends who all convene at minetta's in the west village to celebrate a reality show called who wants to marry a multi-millionaire airs to enormous ratings the contest pits fifty women one from each state against each other for the chance to marry a millionaire they've never met at the end of the show the bride is chosen and marries the millionaire right then and there walking off the set with a three-carat diamond and tens of thousands of dollars in wedding presents because bloomsbury usa is a small office in new york you negotiate your contract with the uk office which means by fax and the old routine you used to employ to communicate with the belgian au pair resumes this time with the woman in the contracts office in london your colleagues at ober help you negotiate a fair contract and the back-and-forth with london is nothing but cordial there's some question as to whether or not the millionaire from the reality show is actually a millionaire and it comes to light that the millionaire is using a fake name and his former girlfriend had to file a restraining order against him when she ended their relationship bloomsbury uk decides to publish a british edition of we're so famous in the summer and you're assigned a british editor as well mostly to work on the cover the bride of the millionaire wants the marriage annulled and tells everyone that the relationship was not consummated on the honeymoon all the police officers who riddled the immigrant reaching for his wallet with forty-one bullets are acquitted the rapper puff daddy pleads not guilty to charges he tried to bribe his driver into saying the gun used at the nightclub shooting was his the video producer for atlantic records that you met through your friend the former drummer–turned–writer has offices in midtown near harold ober and she invites you over for lunch in the atlantic records cafeteria and you can't believe the smorgasbord available for pennies on the dollar to those who can afford otherwise your editor takes you to lunch to celebrate your signing the contract and you meet for hangar steaks at les halles a parisian brasserie on park avenue near your editor's office in the flatiron building proximity is not the only connection the restaurant enjoys its executive chef is anthony bourdain another bloomsbury author bourdain brings your hangar steaks and chats for a bit before disappearing back into the kitchen his ponytail the last you see of him your editor who resembles a young john f kennedy jr reiterates his praise for we're so famous and you touch on what's ahead in terms of copyediting and designing the cover and asking writers for blurbs you say you think you can get a few blurbs easily and he leaves that task to you the marriage between the bride and the millionaire is finally annulled after a late night of drinking with your friend who is writing the bar memoir you're stranded on the subway platform far from brooklyn with a sudden urge to urinate you drift away from your friends and the crowds of people walking into the tunnel a little ways and relieve yourself when you walk back into the light a half a dozen or so off-duty police officers also waiting for the train pull out the badges they're wearing around their necks and you're arrested and released with a ticket on the spot much to the amusement of your friends your editor commissions a photo shoot in a limousine with two girls dressed in '80s clothes for the cover of your book the first part of the advance payment from bloomsbury arrives and you write a check to the southern lawyer back in phoenix who loaned you the money he couldn't be more surprised to be repaid so quickly a cuban boy whose mother drowned trying to cross the waters into florida and who has been staying with his relatives in miami is seized and returned to cuba to the boy's father the tug-of-war between the united states and cuba over the boy won by cuba you concoct the idea of an oral biography of bret easton ellis much like george plimpton's book about edie sedgwick you plan to talk to all of bret's friends and contemporaries excited about the idea you bring it to bret who smiles and assents to your exploring it telling you to keep him posted the rapper eminem is arrested twice once for assaulting a man he witnessed kissing his estranged wife outside of a nightclub and another time for waving a gun at rival rappers insane clown posse the copyediting of your book commences you're given a printout of your manuscript with queries from the copyeditor most of which you can answer easily but one about the spelling of one of the singers in bananarama you're not sure about and you hunt through some local record stores for the answer a concorde flight takes off from paris and crashes immediately killing everyone on board an agent in the midst of a divorce rents an empty office at harold ober and you ask him to represent the oral biography of bret easton ellis and he agrees to send it around for you the rapper eminem records a song wherein he describes killing his estranged wife you ask bret for a blurb for we're so famous and he gives you one that nails what you're trying to convey jaime clarke pulls off a sympathetic act of sustained male imagination entering the minds of innocent teenage girls dreaming of fame a glibly surreal world where the only thing wanted is notoriety and all you really desire leads to celebrity and where stardom is the only point of reference what's new about this novel is how unconsciously casual the characters' drives are this lust is as natural to them as being american it's almost a birthright imagine britney spears narrating the day of the locust as a gentle fable and you'll get the idea your editor loves the blurb too and says he'll put it on the cover ditto the british editor and the british edition eminem's estranged wife attends his concert on his promise that he won't perform the song he wrote about her but he does anyway and she leaves distraught getting in a car wreck on the way home once home she tries to commit suicide by slitting her wrists the british cover for we're so famous is a beautiful shot of the hollywood sign traced over in pink the writer and now raconteur jonathan ames also gives you a blurb darkly and pinkly comic this is the story of a trio of teenage american girls and their pursuit of the three big m's of american life music movies and murder this is an impressive debut by a talented young novelist everyone is afraid of contracting the west nile virus which is spread through mosquitoes the bride who had her tv marriage to the millionaire annulled poses for playboy the last blurb for we're so famous comes from bob shacochis a national book award–winning author you know from bennington like a make-up artist jaime clarke is a master illusionist in his deft hands emptiness seems full teenage pathos appears sassy and charming we're so famous is a blithe highly entertaining indictment of the permanent state of adolescence that trademarks our culture a made-for-tv world where innocence is hardly a virtue ambition barely a value system eminem files for divorce from his estranged wife and she sues him for ten million dollars for defaming her in the song he wrote about her all of the pieces that constitute the first issue of post road are gathered by the editors and your friend who runs the print shop at memorial sloan kettering and who is also the theater editor and publisher begins laying out the magazine you head to the print shop every day after your job at harold ober to help with the design and printing all of the editors who can congregate at the print shop after hours and help collate and bind too you come home to your apartment and find all the furniture in your bedroom gone having forgotten that it belongs to your roommate's friend and so you cobble together the couch cushions for the night before arranging for a new mattress to be delivered working the switchboard at harold ober late on a friday afternoon before you're supposed to hop a train to visit your friend who works for the paris review at her parents' house in the hamptons you answer a call for the divorced agent who is soliciting editors with your proposed oral biography of bret easton ellis the divorced agent is gone for the weekend and you say so and the caller reveals himself to be a reporter for new york magazine looking to track you down for a comment about an article they're going to run about bret refusing to cooperate with the oral biography all your nerves are snapping as you pretend not to have any contact information to give and you get off the phone as quickly as possible brooding on the train about what's going on if you've offended bret in some way worried that you've done something terrible the whole episode threatens the nice weekend you've planned with your friend who works for the paris review and when she picks you up at the train station she senses something and you blurt it all out she offers to help says she has a friend from college who is a hacker and who can get into the new york magazine server you say yes please and after an hour or so you're holding a printout of the article new york magazine is going to publish called bret easton ellis evades history which reads bret easton ellis has always had a knack for getting press but young writers looking to hitch their wagons to his publicity mule should look elsewhere the american psycho author tells us he is refusing to cooperate with an oral history of his life and work being written by fellow bennington alum jamie clarke according to inside.com clarke intends to interview such literary folk as tama janowitz jay mcinerney and joan didion so why won't ellis touch the project with a ten-foot pen a friend of his tells us he just isn't in the mood but another tipster says that ellis was put off when he found out that a character in clarke's upcoming debut novel we're so famous is bryan metro a character from ellis's the informers more bad news for clarke who could not be reached for comment comes from an editor at a top publisher who's been pitched the project we saw the proposal and we were like no it does not make any sense to do this says the insider explaining that ellis is too young for his bio to make a good read the literary biographies that work are about the range of a person's life unless you've got a writer in an older stage it's hard to see any evolution well we're sure clarke will dig up something you

vow to avoid bret for a while and when you do see him again you ask
if he saw the article and he smiles and says he saw it and that's that
a pop culture magazine called shout publishes an early excerpt of
we're so famous by arrangement with bloomsbury usa and the
magazine editor asks if you want to contribute nonfiction and you
pitch an article about how the rapper tupac shakur's fans believe he
isn't really dead and will rise again on a date in the future you're not
much of a rap fan so you consult your youngest brother who is to get
the facts straight shout loves the idea and runs the piece the
whitewater investigation against president clinton closes without
any charges being leveled the first issue of post road comes out and
you arrange back-to-back parties in bars in new york city and boston
to celebrate both attended by most of the editors and a lot of writers
who welcome the magazine into the literary world mister rogers
from mister rogers' neighborhood is diagnosed with stomach cancer
and announces the end of his show he'll tape a handful of episodes
to wind the show down that will air in the coming months your
roommates sit around the television giggling about how they voted
for ralph nader for president but then disbelief sets in as they watch
the election results roll in it all coming down to which candidate
vice president al gore or texas governor george w bush wins the state
of florida most of the television networks call florida for gore but a
couple of hours later they retract and think maybe the votes mostly
belong to bush early the next morning gore calls bush to concede
but on his way to thank his supporters his aides tell him that florida
is too close to call so he doubles back to his campaign headquarters
and calls bush to rescind his concession because the margin of
victory for bush is so slim the state of florida initiates a recall next
day the popular vote totals are released for the election and gore has
about 150,000 more votes than bush but neither has enough electoral
votes to win gore asks for a hand count in some counties but the
results have to be certified within a week and the secretary of state
admits they'll be lucky to make the deadline two days later bush
wants an injunction to stop the hand recounts next day the hand

counting expands to more counties next day a judge rejects bush's injunction to stop the hand recounts one of the larger democratic counties votes against hand recounting next day florida officials vote to delay further recounts until they can clarify if they have the right to undertake the recounts also a judge in palm beach hears a case about poor ballot design which might've led some voters wanting to vote for gore to actually vote for a third-party candidate the secretary of state certifies the election results in bush's favor next day the large democratic county reverses itself and decides to recount the secretary of state files a petition with the florida supreme court to stop recounts bush joins the petition gore threatens to sue for a recount in all counties if bush doesn't accept recounts of the contested counties the florida supreme court denies the request to block recounts the secretary of state says she will not consider returns from counties conducting recounts bush rejects gore's proposal for a statewide recount as well as the suggestion that they meet face-to-face next day bush files an appeal with the federal appeals court in atlanta to stop the recounts in florida gore files a motion in opposition also filing an emergency motion with the state challenging the secretary of state's right to refuse to certify some election results the florida supreme court says the state can go ahead with recounting next day the florida supreme court says the secretary of state may not yet certify results the court of appeals in atlanta denies bush's request to stop the manual recounts next day bush's lead over gore triples when all of the overseas ballots are counted next day another county opts to recount manually next day the florida supreme court hears arguments about whether or not the secretary of state should have to wait for all recounts to certify election results next day the florida supreme court rules in a unanimous decision that recounts may continue and that the totals must be included in the final results all results must be certified in the next five days next day vice presidential candidate dick cheney suffers a mild heart attack and undergoes an operation to place a stent in his narrowing artery bush petitions the u.s. supreme court over the florida surpreme court ruling about counting all ballots a judge in florida says hanging chads cannot be excluded from the recount the county comprising miami votes to halt its manual recount next day gore files papers with the florida supreme court to force the county comprising miami to resume recounting but the court rejects the motion the u.s. supreme court agrees to hear bush's complaints about recounting next day bush drops a lawsuit he filed to force florida to reconsider ballots from overseas military members rejected on technicalities next day the secretary of state denies one county an hour-and-a-half extension of the 5 pm deadline to file totals and thousands of ballots are left uncounted the secretary of state declares bush the winner in florida but there's too much in doubt for it to mean anything five hundred votes separate bush and gore in florida the governor who is george bush's brother certifies the electoral votes next day gore officially contests the election results with the state of florida bush files a motion with the appeals court in atlanta to delay the start of the trial over whether or not florida has the right to recount next day gore asks a county circuit judge to authorize an immediate recount of tens of thousands of disputed ballots the judge wants everything the ballots the voting booths and voting machines brought to his courtroom next day gore and bush file briefs with the united states supreme court over bush's appeal of the florida state supreme court's authorizing selective recounts next day vice presidential candidate dick cheney announces the opening of transition offices funded by private money when the government refuses to release transition funds and office space to bush because of ongoing litigation next day the united states supreme court hears arguments about bush's complaints about the state of florida initiating selective recounts the florida supreme court rejects gore's request to immediately begin hand recounts of tens of thousands of ballots from palm beach and the county comprising miami the court of appeals in atlanta agrees to hear cases brought by private individuals that assert that hand recounts are illegal and unconstitutional the florida circuit judge who had ballots and booths and machines hauled into his courtroom holds a hearing about whether or not the tens of thousands of disputed ballots from palm beach and the county including miami should be recounted by hand two days later the united states supreme court overturns the florida supreme court's decision to restart hand counting and asks for some clarification about the previous deadline for certifying election results the florida circuit judge who had the ballots and booths and machines hauled into his courtroom rules against gore saying recounts aren't necessary in the disputed counties as they're heavily democratic so the totals should stand two days later the appeals court in atlanta denies bush's appeal to throw out manual recounts in some counties next day gore appeals the ruling of the circuit judge who had the ballots and booths and machines hauled into his courtroom to the florida supreme court next day the florida supreme court reverses the circuit judge's ruling and orders statewide manual recounts bush seeks a stay before the recounts can begin and petitions the united states supreme court to intervene next day the florida supreme court refuses bush's stay and begins recounts the appeals court in atlanta also refuses bush's stay but the united states supreme court issues a stay and all manual recounts come to a halt two days later the united states supreme court hears arguments from both bush and gore lawyers on the issue of the recount bush arguing that the recount is a constitutional violation of the equal protection clause because there is no one standard for undertaking said recount and gore argues it's just common sense that the recounting is just to show the will of the people the next day the florida house of representatives approves the twenty-five electors pledged to bush in the afternoon the united states supreme court overturns the florida supreme court's ruling to restart recounting siding with bush that because the recounts are undertaken without a statewide standard for doing so it violates the constitution the next day gore appears on television to concede the election and george w bush becomes president your roommates are beside themselves and get squeamish at various news reports that third-party candidates like the one they voted for likely siphoned off votes for gore the

rapper eminem and his wife reconcile the magazine editor at shout
who ran your piece on the rapper tupac shakur invites you to a party
in chelsea thrown for a new magazine edited by the daughter of the
rolling stones guitarist keith richards neither of you knowing in
advance that keith richards is going to be at the party the magazine
editor says oh my god when he spots the recognizable silhouette of
the legendary guitarist you tell him he should go say something to
richards and the magazine editor admits the thought makes him so
nervous he might vomit you roam a large circle around richards just
to check him out and notice the subtle tabs his two bodyguards keep
on you and anyone else who approaches richards's immediate area
you don't really know anything about the rolling stones and so the
glimpse of richards is just a curiosity once an editor you met at bret
easton ellis's christmas party said he was casting about for a writer
to write a piece about how the rolling stones were the worst band
ever and you volunteered for the assignment dropping it when you
mentioned the idea to one of your colleagues at harold ober and he
looked at you gravely and said you should not write such an article
the foreign-rights agent at ober announces that he's leaving
publishing and he advocates for you to have his old job which entails
securing foreign-rights deals on behalf of ober clients also flying to
germany for the annual rights fair the job pays much more than
you're making and you covet the idea of being a kind of agent
without being a full-fledged literary agent but your boss calls you in
to tell you that you're not getting the job and after three years at the
agency you're to remain an assistant you're disappointed but don't
say so and decide to go part-time to work the other angle writing
another novel but you and your roommates are notified that your
apartment building is going to be gutted and renovated to
accommodate the gentrification of williamsburg and the thought of
trying to find yet another apartment coupled with what seems like
your fading status at harold ober goads you into throwing in the
towel you reluctantly give notice at work and sell what few belongings
you have sitting on the bus to the airport you can feel the slow

unwinding of your life in new york you know you'll be back to
celebrate the publication of we're so famous in the spring but outside
of that you wonder if you'll ever see new york again a place that's felt
more like home than any other place you've lived but now you're just
one of the many people who have come to the city full of ambition
only to be bounced back out you move in with your father in his new
house back in arizona committed to finishing another novel one
that you hope will lead you back to new york you still have a couple
of thousand dollars left from your advance for we're so famous and
hope that perhaps more money will come in maybe from sales of
foreign editions or even film options but for the moment you write
eight hours a day on the new book about three characters on a
scavenger hunt through bars in new york your editor faxes over the
first review of we're so famous by publishers weekly a trade magazine
for publishers and booksellers publishers weekly reviews usually
setting the pace for how many and what kind of reviews a book will
get the publishers weekly review is as harsh as you imagine it can get
in its attempt to skewer our obsession with celebrity culture this
trifle of a tale about three teenage girls and their quest for fame and
fortune only manages to injure itself narrated in three parts the
novel follows the exploits of paque stella and daisy talentless
teenagers from phoenix ariz with an overwhelming desire for fame
obsessed with the british girl group bananarama paque and daisy
are avid '80s aficionados the two record an amateur single that gains
notoriety when they are linked to a local murder case but this plot
line is abandoned and their singing career goes nowhere following a
disastrous live performance stella a struggling actress living in
hollywood works in a dinner theater reenacting celebrity deaths her
obsession with her new boyfriend an actor who can't get beyond
failed television pilots paque and daisy join her in hollywood to
work on a no-budget movie with a no-name director will paque and
daisy hit the big time will stella's stalking of bad-boy rocker bryan
metro bear fruit will readers be at all amused by the book's incessant
name-dropping pop culture factoids and the postmodern trick of

slipping screenplays and faux fan letters into the narrative not likely although those who find nick hornby and bret easton ellis too challenging might be engaged for a moment or two satire needs to be smarter than its subject and unfortunately this fable is neither wicked nor clever enough to wade out from the shallows it purports to spoof a blurb from ellis probably won't do much to boost sales after the first 15 minutes and it's hard to tell who the intended audience is readers under 30 won't be familiar with much of the '80s arcana and those over 30 won't have the patience for the puerile protagonists your editor says to give him a call and you do and he laughs the review off saying it must be an old girlfriend but the nastiness of the review does feel personal and you can't help but wonder if it's someone you know new york city is full of wannabe writers many of them taking jobs as critics and while you don't care about a bad review you can't shake the tone from your head you feel strongly that whoever wrote it should have to sign his or her name to it that publishers weekly shouldn't be publishing anonymous reviews if someone feels strongly about a book one way or the other shouldn't do so behind a curtain it shouldn't be done behind a curtain also the review mentions bret easton ellis twice which makes you suspect he's the real target of the reviewer's disdain you immediately recall an episode at harold ober where the editor of the los angeles review of books called the agent of one of ober's authors who publicly hated an author with a new book out the editor wanted to hire the ober author to review the author he hated a setup the ober author rightly declined but the fact that the editor initiated the request spooked you around that time you'd been reading a memoir by the long-dead legendary new york times critic anatole broyard who joyfully confessed that it was the job of the critic to bring writers down a notch which he had done time and again all of it swirling in your head as you brooded about the publishers weekly review for we're so famous the review would likely kill any other reviewers' interest in the book you imagine you are desperate to know the name of the reviewer and wonder how you can find out your friend who worked for the paris review with the hacker friend wouldn't be able to find out because the reviewer's name is likely not filed electronically you hatch a plan a stunt one that at first sounds ludicrous but as you consider it more and more you realize that even if it doesn't reveal the name of the reviewer it will at least raise the profile of your novel and if you know anything it's that a raised profile for whatever reason is better than naught so without telling anyone what you're going to do you send an e-mail to everyone at publishers weekly offering the last thousand dollars of your advance money for the name of the reviewer you also openly cc all the media outlets you can think of and press send before you can talk yourself out of doing it you sleep fitfully that night expecting the time difference in new york to bring replies early in the morning but your barren inbox is a sign either that something is afoot or that no one cares you spend the morning rationalizing what you've done you don't care what people think about you personally all the moving around as a kid erased that from your makeup over the years and you have no agent to disappoint your friends will stick by you you hope your family is family so when your editor calls and asks you what in the world is going on your heart sinks not realizing that publishers weekly would place a call over to bloomsbury usa your editor has been your champion all the way through taking a chance on you and your book and now you've embarrassed him and probably gotten him in trouble with his colleagues something you didn't consider even for a moment mortification sets in and you apologize to him but he's already written you off you can tell and you're in the quagmire of your own making by yourself the publicist at bloomsbury usa calls and asks you not to answer any of the interview requests that are coming in about the bounty and you say you'll do whatever she wants you to forwarding the requests that filter into your inbox straight to her so she can issue a no comment the rapper puff daddy changes his name to p diddy the magazine salon writes a piece about your row with publishers weekly called when authors attack you fly to san diego for a week to meet your friend from new york who is writing the bar memoir who is visiting his friend a hatter who owns a chain of successful hat shops in southern california the music magazine spin publishes a nice short review of we're so famous which you see in a record store in san diego when you return to phoenix the publishers weekly thing seems like a dream until a friend forwards you a piece from time magazine called poor sport disparaging you and what you've done that the journalist is allowed to rail against you without comment from you seems an injustice but you're trying to salvage anything you can of your relationship with your editor and bloomsbury usa a famous hollywood agent becomes your film agent and you know that his interest is a result of the thing with publishers weekly you bounce to new york for a party celebrating the release of the second issue of post road happy to have the distraction you spend a few days seeing friends in new york before taking the bus to boston where there's a second post road party your publicist at bloomsbury usa wants you to speak with a journalist writing a piece about the publishers weekly thing and you agree the journalist starts off by mentioning the blurb for we're so famous from bob shacochis saying that he hates shacochis's work and you wonder what kind of setup you're in for a more studied approach comes from the novelist kurt andersen on his radio show studio 360 finally you hear some agree with you that reviews should not be written anonymously a point that's been lost in the maelstrom you give your first public reading from we're so famous at newtonville books outside of boston a bookstore owned by a friend of your friend from bennington and it's a comfort to see so many friendly faces from bennington in the crowd including some of your former teachers the next day the village voice runs a long favorable review of we're so famous which makes your reaction to the publishers weekly review look like an overreaction you travel back to new york as the official publication date nears for a scheduled reading at the astor place barnes & noble the book party will be a few days later and so your entire family flies out arriving at barnes & noble in cabs from the airport just as the reading is about to start you don't see your editor in the crowd and are bummed out that he's probably too mad at you to attend you begin reading to the crowd of friends and some people you don't know and when you look up from the podium during the reading you see the actress molly ringwald cutting through the crowd finding a place in the corner after the reading you're relieved to find your editor in the back of the room though your interaction with him is a bit awkward before you can launch into an apology about the whole thing and explain your side molly ringwald appears and it's clear they are a couple and all else is washed away in pleasantries the editor stops by the book party which you've arranged at a ukrainian social club in the east village with the help of your friend who is writing a bar memoir and who is married to a ukrainian your friend from college the fitzgerald fan drives up and your family is there and you take a moment to appreciate everyone you care about being in the same room at the same moment you bounce back to arizona the next day and drive to tucson for a sparsely attended reading at your alma mater your former teachers attending one of them saying you didn't waste any time which you think is a compliment but who knows you bounce to los angeles driving through the desert with your father staying in a pastel-colored hotel near the borders in westwood where you're scheduled to read when you and your father check in there's a party of some kind in the lobby bar and you see the actor who played crocodile dundee raising a glass at your reading at borders the next day no one shows up save for one former bennington classmate who sits next to your father but as the reading is about to begin the bennington classmate waltzes through the spacious bookstore and gathers up a few souls whom she deposits in the front row you start reading and a half a dozen men in expensive suits file in and stand at the back agents from the office of the hollywood agent handling the film rights for we're so famous you say a quick hello when it's over and they hightail it out as quickly as they arrived you land back in phoenix the small publicity tour for the novel done entertainment weekly publishes an unfavorable review of we're so famous and you

smile when you think of the bad reviews they've written about bret
easton ellis's books over the years and when the unimpressed new
york times review appears it hardly matters though there's vindication
in the fact that the times reviewed the book at all as they tend not
to review paperback originals a victory of sorts you take a data entry
job at your mother's medical billing business as the last of your
money is gone bloomsbury usa sends a rejection for your new novel
the one about the scavenger hunt and the tilt-a-whirl finally finally
finally comes to a rest an intern in washington dc goes missing and
the congressman from her district in california is questioned the
actor robert blake's wife is found murdered in the passenger seat of
his car he ran back into the italian restaurant where they'd dined to
retrieve his gun which had fallen out of his jacket to put a coda on
the thing with publishers weekly you go on a local radio morning
show and announce that you're donating all the royalties from we're
so famous to a local literacy group it comes out that robert blake's
wife would send nude photos of herself to men as a means of
supporting herself she also ran ads in magazines seeking
companionship and then asking men for money which supported
her lifestyle and gave her enough money to move to los angeles to
pursue a film career that didn't pan out though it allowed her access
to celebrities including marlon brando's son whom she wrote to in
prison after he was convicted of killing his sister's husband after his
release she began dating brando's son though she was also dating
robert blake and when she became pregnant she thought the child
was brando's son's but a paternity test revealed it was blake's he
married her and moved her and the child into the guesthouse of his
home the local paper the phoenix new times publishes an in-depth
profile about you which your friends see and you stop to wonder if
your old high school girlfriend now married sees it too and all of
that feels like a lifetime ago you bounce back to new york city and
drive with friends up to bennington for an alumni weekend and feel
some love for your novel which though it's recently published feels
like another time period you marvel at the fact that it's been only

four years since you graduated you spend a couple of days on cape
cod with your bennington friend from boston and his family his
father the former dean of harvard taking in that your friend and his
family have been like a second family to you through the years of
bouncing between new york and boston and you feel wistful on the
flight back to phoenix bloomsbury publishes the british edition of
we're so famous and there are some nice notices you receive an
e-mail out of the blue from a record producer in london asking for
your address and a few weeks later an envelope arrives with a british
copy of your novel signed by bananarama after denying it for months
the congressman from the district of the disappeared intern admits
that he was having an affair with her but that he knows nothing
about what happened to her madonna announces her first tour in
over a decade the drowned world tour and you think that about says
it all you convince the band fuzzy who appears in we're so famous to
go on a tour of colleges with you in the fall and set about using your
ample free time looking at maps calculating costs locating cheap
hotels the idea that the tour will coincide with the start of the fall
semester inspires you to contact some college english departments
for help in arranging appearances but because it's summer you don't
get a lot of feedback and the idea of touring college campuses fizzles
you're chagrined to learn that the film rights to your novel are being
shopped selectively when a small producer asks for a copy and your
hollywood agent won't send it or even consider the producer the
populist in you fires up and with the help of your brothers you create
a listing on ebay offering up the film rights to we're so famous to the
highest bidder you also fax all the production companies in
hollywood and beyond about the auction your hollywood agent calls
enraged demanding that you halt what you're up to but you don't
listen don't care there's nothing anyone can say at this point that will
influence how you behave the singer aaliyah is killed when her
private plane is overloaded with people and equipment and drops
into the ocean right after takeoff the last episode of mister rogers'
neighborhood airs the monday you targeted for the start of your

college campus tour passes and you're spent all out of ideas for promoting yourself and your novel and then the unreal becomes real when you wake up the following morning and your father says there's been an aviation accident in new york city and you watch the city you love the only real home you've ever known crumble and burn and people stop thinking about themselves at least for the moment while the man who gave away all of those free gum balls so long ago is put in charge of retaliating against those who ruined that part of new york and a lot of people's lives forever but it doesn't take long for everyone to wonder how long is appropriate before it is okay to resume the intense investigation of the insignificant and welcome the comfort of the trivial back into our lives

Jaime Clarke is a graduate of the University of Arizona and holds an MFA from Bennington College. He is the author of the novels *We're So Famous, Vernon Downs, World Gone Water,* and *Garden Lakes;* editor of the anthologies *Don't You Forget About Me: Contemporary Writers on the Films of John Hughes, Conversations with Jonathan Lethem,* and *Talk Show: On the Couch with Contemporary Writers;* and co-editor of the anthologies *No Near Exit: Writers Select Their Favorite Work from Post Road Magazine* (with Mary Cotton) and *Boston Noir 2: The Classics* (with Dennis Lehane and Mary Cotton). He is a founding editor of the literary magazine *Post Road,* now published at Boston College, and co-owner, with his wife, of Newtonville Books, an independent bookstore in Boston.

www.jaimeclarke.com

Praise for VERNON DOWNS

"*Vernon Downs* is a gripping, hypnotically written and unnerving look at the dark side of literary adulation. Jaime Clarke's tautly suspenseful novel is a cautionary tale for writers and readers alike—after finishing it, you may start to think that J.D. Salinger had the right idea after all."

—TOM PERROTTA, author of *Election*, *Little Children*, and *The Leftovers*

"Moving and edgy in just the right way. Love (or lack of) and Family (or lack of) is at the heart of this wonderfully obsessive novel."

—GARY SHTEYNGART, author of *Super Sad True Love Story*

"All strong literature stems from obsession. *Vernon Downs* belongs to a tradition that includes Nicholson Baker's *U and I*, Geoff Dyer's *Out of Sheer Rage*, and—for that matter—*Pale Fire*. What makes Clarke's excellent novel stand out isn't just its rueful intelligence, or its playful semi-veiling of certain notorious literary figures, but its startling sadness. *Vernon Downs* is first rate."

—MATTHEW SPECKTOR, author of *American Dream Machine*

"An engrossing novel about longing and impersonation, which is to say, a story about the distance between persons, distances within ourselves. Clarke's prose is infused with music and intelligence and deep feeling."

—CHARLES YU, author of *Sorry Please Thank You*

"*Vernon Downs* is a fascinating and sly tribute to a certain fascinating and sly writer, but this novel also perfectly captures the lonely distortions of a true obsession."

—DANA SPIOTTA, author of *Stone Arabia*

"*Vernon Downs* is a brilliant meditation on obsession, art, and celebrity. Charlie Marten's mounting fixation with the titular Vernon is not only driven by the burn of heartbreak and the lure of fame, but also a lost young man's struggle to locate his place in the world. *Vernon Downs* is an intoxicating novel, and Clarke is a dazzling literary talent."

—LAURA VAN DEN BERG, author of *The Isle of Youth*

Praise for WORLD GONE WATER

"Charlie Martens will make you laugh. More, he'll offend and shock you while making you laugh. Even trickier: he'll somehow make you like him, root for him, despite yourself and despite him. This novel travels into the dark heart of male/female relations and yet there is tenderness, humanity, hope. Jaime Clarke rides what is a terribly fine line between hero and antihero. Read and be astounded."

—AMY GRACE LOYD, author of *The Affairs of Others*

"Funny and surprising, *World Gone Water* is terrific fun to read and, as a spectacle of bad behavior, pretty terrifying to contemplate."

—ADRIENNE MILLER, author of *The Coast of Akron*

"Jaime Clarke's *World Gone Water* is so fresh and daring, a necessary book, a barbaric yawp that revels in its taboo: the sexual and emotional desires of today's hetero young man. Clarke is a sure and sensitive writer, his lines are clean and carry us right to the tender heart of his lovelorn hero, Charlie Martens. This is the book Hemingway and Kerouac would want to read. It's the sort of honesty in this climate that many of us aren't brave enough to write."

—TONY D'SOUZA, author of *The Konkans*

"Charlie Martens is my favorite kind of narrator, an obsessive yearner whose commitment to his worldview is so overwhelming that the distance between his words and the reader's usual thinking gets clouded fast. *World Gone Water* will draw you in, make you complicit, and finally leave you both discomfited and thrilled."

—MATT BELL, author of *In the House upon the Dirt between the Lake and the Woods*

Praise for GARDEN LAKES

"It takes some nerve to revisit a bulletproof classic, but Jaime Clarke does so, with elegance and a cool contemporary eye, in this cunningly crafted homage to *Lord of the Flies*. He understands all too well the complex psychology of boyhood, how easily the insecurities and power plays slide into mayhem when adults look the other way."

—JULIA GLASS, National Book Award-winning author of *Three Junes*

"As tense and tight and pitch-perfect as Clarke's narrative of the harrowing events at *Garden Lakes* is, and as fine a meditation it is on Golding's novel, what deepens this book to another level of insight and artfulness is the parallel portrait of Charlie Martens as an adult, years after his fateful role that summer, still tyrannized, paralyzed, tangled in lies, wishing for redemption, maybe fated never to get it. Complicated and feral, *Garden Lakes* is thrilling, literary, and smart as hell."

—PAUL HARDING, Pulitzer Prize-winning author of *Tinkers*

"Jaime Clarke reminds us that if the banality of evil is indeed a viable truth, its seeds are most likely sewn among adolescent boys."

—BRAD WATSON, author of *Aliens in the Prime of Their Lives*

"In the flawlessly imagined *Garden Lakes*, Jaime Clarke pays homage to *Lord of the Flies* and creates his own vivid, inadvertently isolated community. As summer tightens its grip, and adult authority recedes, his boys gradually reveal themselves to scary and exhilarating effect. In the hands of this master of suspense and psychological detail, the result is a compulsively readable novel."

—MARGOT LIVESEY, author of *The Flight of Gemma Hardy*

"Smart, seductive, and suggestively sinister, *Garden Lakes* is a disturbingly honest look at how our lies shape our lives and destroy our communities. Read it: Part three in one of the best literary trilogies we have."

—SCOTT CHESHIRE, author of *High as the Horses' Bridles*

Praise for WE'RE SO FAMOUS

"Jaime Clarke pulls off a sympathetic act of sustained male imagination: entering the minds of innocent teenage girls dreaming of fame. A glibly surreal world where the only thing wanted is notoriety and all you really desire leads to celebrity and where stardom is the only point of reference. What's new about this novel is how unconsciously casual the characters' drives are. This lust is as natural to them as being American—it's almost a birthright."

—BRET EASTON ELLIS

"Daisy, Paque, and Stella want. They want to be actresses. They want to be in a band. They want to be models. They want to be famous, damn it. And so . . . they each tell their story of forming a girl group, moving to LA, and flirting with fame. Clarke doesn't hate his antiheroines—he just views them as by-products of the culture: glitter-eyed, vacant, and cruel. The satire works, sliding down as silvery and toxic as liquid mercury."

—ENTERTAINMENT WEEKLY

"Jaime Clarke is a masterful illusionist; in his deft hands, emptiness seems full, teenage pathos appears sassy and charming. *We're So Famous* is a blithe, highly entertaining indictment of the permanent state of adolescence that trademarks our culture, a made-for-TV world where innocence is hardly a virtue, ambition barely a value system."

—BOB SHACOCHIS

"Clarke seems to have created a crafty book of bubble letters to express his anger, sending off a disguised Barbie mail bomb that shows how insipid and money-drenched youth culture can be."

—VILLAGE VOICE

What Was the Question Again?

What Was the Question Again?

Charlie Martens

Roundabout Press   2022

I. What Was the Question Again?

I WAS AT A PARTY ONCE, YEARS AGO, WHEN THE MOVIE *MAGNOLIA* was on everyone's lips, and someone across the room started waxing on and on about what a great film it was. I'd spent the better part of a Martin Luther King Jr. holiday watching it, and it has some nice moments, but more interestingly the film provides a fun and easy litmus test to weed out the pretentious in any crowd. Just ask, "What's up at the end with the frogs falling from the sky?" Then count up the silent but pitying looks and you'll know who is who.

The reason I remember that it was Martin Luther King Jr. Day is that it was over a hundred degrees that day, hot for Arizona in January, the earliest in recorded time that the desert had boiled over. So a darkened theater seemed the perfect cloak from the heat. After the showing, I lingered in the bathroom until the next showing and watched it again just to be indoors. The theater was the Valley Art, an old pink and neon Art Deco gem on Mill Avenue in Tempe dating back to the 1930s. For most of the time I lived in Arizona, it was the only place besides maybe Ciné Capri in Phoenix where you could see interesting movies.

Tempe is the college town outside Phoenix that Arizona State University ("Go Sun Devils!") calls home. Around the corner and up the street, more toward campus, is Sun Devil Stadium, the collegiate arena where ASU's football team does battle. Way back when I was in high school, the Irish rock band U2 played a couple

of sold-out concerts back-to-back at Sun Devil Stadium so they could film scenes for their rockumentary, *Rattle and Hum*. Tickets to the show were five dollars, and most of us attended the show both nights. Those of us who grew up in the desert in the late '80s believed deeply in the myths promoted on U2's album *The Joshua Tree* and, further, believed the album was about us collectively. Even when I close my eyes now, the haunting keyboard intro that gives way to the brain-tingling guitar riff evokes the desert after a rainstorm, or the smell of orange blossoms after midnight, in summer, when it was cool enough to go for a drive with the windows down.

The Joshua Tree began the period of time when the lead singer, Bono, became Saint Bono, and while you sometimes laughed at his pretentiousness, you were still a member of the congregation. On the previous album, *The Unforgettable Fire*, Bono famously muffed the time of day Martin Luther King Jr. was killed, saying it was early morning when in fact it was just after six o'clock at night. So he was still human, in his way. There are plenty of song lyrics that aren't factually true anyway. "Thunder only happens when it's rainin'." "Only the good die young." The notion that doves can cry . And then there are completely untrue lyrics like "Every little thing she does is magic." Or this false chestnut: "I don't care about spots on my apples / Leave me the birds and the bees." Spotted apples are the last ones people reach for at the grocery store. Don't most people sort through the apples, touching each one, looking for those without imperfections? And probably not just apples.

Bono had low-hanging fruit at those two concerts for *Rattle and Hum*. The governor of Arizona, a Mormon used-car salesman who won without garnering a majority of votes, made his first order of business to cancel the Martin Luther King Jr. Day holiday. "Blacks don't need holidays, they need jobs," he said. By the summer a petition to recall the governor was circulating, and Bono encouraged everyone to join the fight. You got the impression that Bono *lived* in Phoenix, that it was personal, such is his gift. He is that mesmerizing personality who looks you in the eye when

he's speaking and later you have dreams about him, and still later it seems strange that he's no longer in your life, save for his voice coming through your speakers.

Ever see that duet Bono did with Frank Sinatra? Think it was for a gimmicky album where Sinatra and other famous artists sang Sinatra classics, but they didn't sing them together—they were actually in separate studios, and the magic of editing made it appear they were singing to each other?

I met a kid in a community college class way back who claimed she had a million-dollar idea for a card game called Who Sucks More? The idea was you'd flip two cards off the deck to reveal a couple of names, X and Y, and the game was for you to argue that X sucked more than Y, or vice versa. I asked how you would score the game to find a winner, and she said *persuasion* would be the judge. The winner would be obvious. I said, "Okay, let's give it a try." She said, "Who sucks more: Sinatra or Streisand?"

I equivocated, secretly hoping to please her, trying to read her expression for a tell about who *she* thought sucked more. But in truth, I knew nothing about Barbra Streisand, except for that people my age thought she was uncool, and sometimes confused her for Bette Midler. I had more of an opinion about Sinatra and opted to argue the case that he sucked more. The Sinatra duets project seemed to me preposterous, and I began my answer with how pathetic it was, but I was surprisingly loquacious on the subject of Sinatra, betraying a lifelong bafflement about ol' Frank's popularity. I went on a pretty solid tear about him being merely a personality, one you either dug or not. The *idea* of Sinatra was more important to fans than any of his dumb songs or his lame attempts at acting. If you were a Sinatra fan, God help you, it was because you liked the insertion of his familiar face and voice into whatever was before you. Sinatra was comfort food for an entire generation, their macaroni and cheese and mashed potato dinner, and though I probably intuited that *every* generation had its equivalent, I tore into Sinatra, the words tripping off my tongue. Then I went for the win with the lines from

the David Mamet film *Heist*:

"'Nobody lives forever.'

"'Frank Sinatra gave it a try.'"

The Empire State Building was lit blue when Sinatra died, a silent tribute. I heard about it a year later, on a brief stay in New York. "New York, New York" blaring from every open bar door. If you can make it there, well. The same drunk nobody who related that bit of trivia in the Black Rabbit said the Empire State Building had also been lit in tribute to Jimmy Stewart, who had died at the age of eighty-nine.

"Who sucks more: Jimmy Stewart or Bing Crosby?" I asked the nobody, who got a horrified look on his face.

"Just kidding," I said, to the nobody's relief.

I consider myself a Jimmy Stewart fan, though I admit he's a personality player like Frank Sinatra. When you watch a Jimmy Stewart movie, you're signing up for Jimmy Stewart's personality over whatever story is being told. There are shades, of course, like Sinatra. Jimmy in *It's a Wonderful Life* is a shade lighter than the Jimmy of, say, *Rope* or *Rear Window*. But it's still Jimmy.

I once got into a heated discussion in a bar in New York with a different set of nobodies about Hitchcock movies, about how great they are, but how every single goddamn one of them has a little thing that drives you crazy.

Take *Vertigo*, for example, which is always at the top of the best-of lists. So much of it is terrific, but in the back half of the film, that part that ties it all together, we're supposed to believe that Judy, poor Judy, was so terrific an actress as the double for the murdered wife that she had to go back to her job as a salesgirl? C'mon, son. That dipshit husband would've had to *pay* her to bring that deception off. He's gonna skate off to Europe and leave her roaming the streets of San Francisco and take a chance that no one would put it together, let alone Jimmy Stewart, a former cop ? Also, it has to be said, a girl with that much talent for deception is probably not a salesgirl. No offense to salesgirls. Hitchcock movies are full of things like that, drive you crazy.

There are no perfect films, I guess. What's the closest? Actually, there's a film that's nearly perfect, and it's Hitchcockian, though it's probably not fashionable to say because it was directed by Roman Polanski. *The Ghost Writer*. Seen it? Every beat, every scene, every character, is perfect. Its only flaws are minimal, like how Ewan McGregor turns left at the New York Store in Provincetown on Cape Cod after getting off the ferry, when that only takes you farther down Commercial Street rather than to Boston, where the OnStar lady is trying to direct him.

I only know that because of my one trip up to Boston, a twenty-dollar bus ride from New York, back in the day. Get on in Chinatown, fall asleep, wake up in Connecticut to pee when the bus stops, maybe grab some McDonald's, watch the landscape go by like a verdant zoetrope until you're deposited in a different Chinatown, one less threatening than before, ride the trolly system in Boston that stands in for a real subway. A friend I'd made in the first days of my first move to New York invited me to come up anytime. Sometimes in life you meet instant friends like these. I boarded the bus as a lark, desperate to escape the city. If you've ever been to New York in the summer, you know it's just tourists and garbage strikes that leave the streets stinking to high heaven.

I'd made the friend at a show at CBGB (this was New York back before every corner had a Starbucks and a Duane Reade pharmacy). Her name slips my mind, but I remember her father was a financier of note. "Financier" is a word that never carries a positive connotation, amiright?

Back in Arizona we had our own infamous financier, Charlie Keating, who was in the papers every day. Keating was a real estate developer who bought Lincoln Savings and Loan in California, and may or may not have tricked senior citizens into investing their life savings in junk bonds, which are high yield but high risk, in order to get cash to invest in his real estate empire. Our guy Charlie was raking in cash and investing it in developments in Arizona, the kind that have grass where there shouldn't be grass, all financed

by Lincoln Savings and Loan, made possible by the government's relaxation of the rules surrounding savings and loans.

Ever press your fingernails into your gums until they bleed? It's an oddly satisfying sensation. After the second *Rattle and Hum* concert in Tempe that December before Christmas, a girl who claimed to be a vampire sat on a stolen futon in an apartment I couldn't find again with a gun to my head and cut herself on her upper arm, under her sleeve, and her boyfriend slurped the blood that ran in tiny rivulets down her arm. When I press my fingernails into my gums and hold them there, I think of the aspiring vampire and wonder what she's up to now, or if she remembers that night.

I shouldn't have said how much I like *The Ghost Writer*. The fact that Roman Polanski's victim, now an adult, defends him is no defense. You can't speak for someone else's pain, but you can speak for yourself, and speaking for myself, the idea of a grown man doing what he did to a thirteen-year-old girl, no matter who he is, or whose house he was at, drives me to the brink. And yes, I've seen *The Ghost Writer* at least a dozen times, and every time I feel guilty about it, and at least a dozen times I've tried to convince myself that if all the actors in the movie thought it was okay to associate themselves with Polanski, it's okay for me to like the movie. Which, of course, is . . . what's the word?

But you have to overlook a lot of stuff to merely function. One foot doesn't get in front of the other if your scorecard is heavily marked up. Forget about the flaws in the films of Hitchcock; by all accounts, he was a questionable human being. What he did to Tippi Hedren? Oh, sorry, what he *allegedly* did. If your coworker behaved in a similar fashion, he or she'd be on trial and you'd be a witness.

Was thinking about that very thing when I was last at Taliesin West, the place in Scottsdale where Frank Lloyd Wright founded a school back in the late 1930s. The American West is famous for those seeking reinvention. Wright was no different. His family had just been murdered by a paranoid Barbadian chef, a tragedy that might've crippled an ordinary life, but even before that he'd created

trouble for himself by abandoning a wife and running off with the wife of a client. On down the line. So the sun-tinted red rocks of the Valley of the Sun must've been a welcome reprieve.

The heavy mythology surrounding Wright—he was essentially a pop star at the end of his life—wants to obscure the inconvenient fact that he might've been an arrogant pseudointellectual. The beaming smile on the tour guide's face faded when I posited just such a question, and before the guide could answer, someone else on the tour, a hayseed from nowhere, made a quip that bailed out the tour guide and I didn't get an answer to my query. The better question, for tour guides everywhere, is this: Why do we generally overlook the terrible personalities of quote-unquote geniuses? Does the world need more brilliant art, books, architecture, what have you, or could it use another decent person? The nervous jackasses among us will be quick to point out that the two aren't mutually exclusive, but what about the preponderance of examples that prove the opposite?

I mean, I dig Frank Lloyd Wright. I've purposely traveled to many of his creations. Stood at Fallingwater. Climbed the pulpit at Unity Temple when I was in Chicago. Looked out at Lake Erie from the windows of the Darwin Martin House in Buffalo. Something about the clean lines of Wright's work appeals to me on a base, childlike level. Have to admit that. And though all the furniture and all the rooms I've stood in, including those at Taliesin, appear wildly uncomfortable for everyday living, they have a movie-set quality that gets the old goose bumps popping.

I shouldn't've said Frank Sinatra sucked more than Barbra Streisand. That was childish. I should've been courageous enough to say that I hated the way fans co-opted Sinatra's music and incorporated it into their personal mythology. Everyone quote-unquote doing it their way. Nauseating. Guessing the same could be true for fans of Streisand, but how would I know?

Or Bob Marley. My innards curdle when I hear the opening notes of any Bob Marley song and my mind shuts down; but upon

reflection, it's not Marley I'm reacting violently to, it's all the white kids I knew in Arizona who sprouted dreadlocks and got high because Bob got high, or adopted Bob as their pot buddy as cover. Or, worse, the plain vanillas without any personality of their own who started smoking pot and listening to Bob Marley to *borrow his personality*.

Know who else is an inveterate pot smoker? You'd never guess, or maybe you would. Rick Steves. Know this motherfucker? Travels the world with nothing more than a backpack slung over his shoulder? If Rick Steves isn't in real life the nicest guy you'd ever want to meet, we are all of us kidding ourselves about our day-to-day realities. It's clear that if you're in Rick Steves's company, nothing bad is going to happen to you. Rick Steves isn't going to find himself in a hot tub at Jack Nicholson's house with a thirteen-year-old girl. Rick Steves isn't going to run off with a friend's wife. Rick Steves is proof of decency. And he can't be the only one. It's hard all of the time not to be overwhelmed by the filth inflicted upon us by the lowest common denominator.

In a game of Who Sucks More? you should pray Rick Steves is always the second choice. The other person undoubtedly sucks more. That's just math.

But Christ, I like the movie *Chinatown*, too. Have seen it as many times or more than *The Ghost Writer*. A thriller about water rights! Nicholson at his finest. Faye Dunaway stealing every scene. John Huston giving a career-capping performance.

But then you're thrown back into the other thing: Roman Polanski at Jack Nicholson's house, where he lived with John Huston's daughter, Anjelica Huston, who wandered into the surely criminal scene of Polanski and the drugged thirteen-year-old girl in the hot tub. All the elements of a compelling film, but also details of a terrible criminal and immoral act.

How much can one person be expected to overlook? And for how long?

Well, but. Polanski pled guilty and actually served more than

a month in prison for his crime and only fled to Europe when the tables were turned on him by the judge overseeing his case, who was shown a photo of Polanski with his arms around some underage girls postconviction. The judge was allegedly a publicity junkie—it was LA, after all—and swore a campaign against Polanski rather than honoring the plea agreement.

Life is full of plausible deniability, but doesn't said deniability say more about the denier than it does about what is denied? An immoral act was committed, without question, and in its attempt to offer justice, the meager justice system, never up to the challenge of regulating what is morally right and wrong, created enough false narratives to provide cover to Polanski, so that three decades later I'm transfixed watching Ewan McGregor, whose ghost writer character is never named, come to grips with the morally reprehensible person whose memoirs he's ghosting.

When you hang a Louie at the New York Store in Provincetown on Cape Cod in the summer, you're treated to a carnival featuring drag queens, homosexuals, and saltwater taffy stores. After hopping off the Chinatown bus, I made the last ferry from the seaport and kicked my feet up on an empty seat while the bow cut a direct line across Massachusetts Bay . My CBGB friend's parents had a house in Provincetown for reasons that are still unknown to me, as the house was, according to my friend, always empty. I never saw the house, though, and before we lost sight of each other that night, we had an unpleasant experience at a darkened bar blaring some of our favorite tunes. The sunlight drained from our eyes as we entered the cool, low space, and when my pupils adjusted, the first thing I noticed was a shirtless man dressed as a centaur, which, hard to believe maybe, was not an out-of-place sight. Of course there'd be a centaur in the bar! My friend and I pulled ourselves up to the wide plank bar and ordered some cold beers. But we'd drunk only half of them before a friend of the centaur's politely let us know that women weren't allowed in the bar. My new friend giggled, as if this custom of the country was an amusement, but I could feel a tightness grip

me. The reservoir of goodwill I'd built up high-fiving drag queens on Commercial Street drained in a sudden rush. I was apoplectic that, having faced discrimination practically everywhere and from everyone, the patrons were practicing reverse discrimination in the Shangri-la built as a celebration of the gay lifestyle.

My friend tried to distract me from my rage, but as the sun began to cast long shadows, she mentioned that the last ferry back to Boston left soon, as if remembering something she'd mentioned earlier, as if that had been the plan all along.

How many people think Martin Luther King Jr. was assassinated in the early morning based on the U2 song, do you think? Not that it matters. The enormity of the act, and the emotions the song conveys about the assassination, are more important. But a century from now, the lyrics may come to stand in for common knowledge, the facts of the history books lost on the general populace. Like the Oliver Stone movie *JFK*. Me and my generation know the movie so well, it's as good as a documentary to us. We believe the CIA and the military-industrial complex were involved. We're sure Lee Harvey Oswald was a patsy. The summation by Kevin Costner as Jim Garrison at the end of the movie beautifully sows the seeds of doubt about an entire generation's understanding of the murder of their president. The line "Who grieves for Lee Harvey Oswald?" feels seditious if you don't fully embrace the movie and its mission to finally solve a generational mystery.

Is it any wonder that baby boomers love conspiracy theories? The assassination of President Kennedy was the first chapter in the novel of that generation's upbringing. Sirhan Sirhan may or may not have assassinated Robert F. Kennedy in the kitchen of the Ambassador Hotel five years after his brother was gunned down in Dallas; Martin Luther King Jr. was shot the same year; the United States landed men on the moon (maybe) the following year; then came the terrible cover-up by President Richard Nixon of the markedly lame crime committed at the Watergate office complex. Too many conspiracies for one generation to bear.

Paul Harvey, the radio star, lived out most of his final years in a mansion at the Biltmore Estates in the Camelback Corridor in Phoenix, his red Ferrari sometimes parked in the driveway. It was rumored he had a studio somewhere in the mansion where he could record his famous broadcast, telling everyone "the rest of the story." No small wonder that his audience was so large, those who were sure there was always more to the story, something that wasn't being said, a conspiracy of silence.

Up the hill from Paul Harvey's estate is the Wrigley Mansion, built by the chewing gum magnate back in the day. Ever hear the one about how chewing gum stays in your stomach for seven years? The children of the baby boomers carrying on the tradition. A penny dropped from the Empire State Building can kill you. *Disney on Ice* is a nod to the fact that Walt Disney is cryogenically frozen somewhere, waiting to make his triumphant return. Elvis Presley once stayed at the Wrigley Mansion. Who sucks more: Elvis Presley or Rick Steves?

The crown jewel of the Biltmore Estates is the Arizona Biltmore Hotel. Many of the expensive homes line the hotel's golf course. There's a common misconception that Frank Lloyd Wright designed the hotel, because it bears a resemblance to his previous works. Wright *was* a consultant on the hotel for a few months, but he is not the architect of record. That honor goes to a draftsman who worked for Wright. But the Biltmore Hotel has been Wrightified over the years. A stained-glass window fabricated from a design of Wright's was installed at some point. And then of course the various bars and restaurants throughout the hotel are named with a nod to ol' Frank. Too bad for what's his name, who actually designed the hotel.

The worst moment of my life occurred in a hotel. Nothing like the Arizona Biltmore Hotel. Farthest thing from it. A hotel off the westbound I-10, past the I-17 interchange. I met a girl, Madeline, the summer after high school while working as a caddy for the golf club at the Arizona Biltmore. Her father golfed at the Biltmore, and she would sometimes sit in the clubhouse snacking on Cheez-Its

and Diet Pepsi, playing solitaire with a deck of Uno cards, while I followed her father around for eighteen holes, pointing out his ball in the rough, sometimes pretending to discover it on the lip between the fairway and the course. Madeline always seemed out of reach, lost in her own thoughts, but she laughed at a random aside I made while passing her table and we became fast friends.

We both liked the new AM alternative music station, KUKQ, and she somehow snagged us tickets to the first Q-Fest, a music festival the station was hosting at Big Surf, a cheesy water park in Tempe that featured a wave pool. They claimed it was the *first* wave pool in America, which seems like a pointless distinction. Though apparently when it first opened, you really could surf on surfboards, before someone realized that might be dangerous and put the kibosh on it. Madeline said Pink Floyd once played Big Surf, in the '70s, and I teased her about secretly being a fan of the Q's sister station, KUPD, which played hard rock. The morning DJ at KUPD was a bit of a local legend. People called him the Morning Mayor and turned out for concerts by the band he fronted, the Sex Machine Band. The Morning Mayor was always courting controversy and was an early prototypical shock jock, perhaps. One of the bits his fans couldn't get enough of was a segment called "Spelling with Darnell." Darnell was a semiliterate character who would successfully spell a word like "dictates" and then use it in a sentence: "I asked my girlfriend how my dictates."

The lineup for the first Q-Fest included just four bands: the Red Hot Chili Peppers; Mary's Danish; the Sidewinders, a local band from Tucson who later had to change their name to the Sand Rubies after another band called the Sidewinders sued and won; and Camper Van Beethoven. Big Surf could hold only about ten thousand people, and Madeline bumped into a few people she knew, introducing me as her friend. I wanted to be more than friends and endeavored to be as clever and funny as I could as an audition to becoming her boyfriend. The problem was she was cleverer and funnier, by far, and I could feel myself being relegated to sidekick.

I finally made my move when Madeline expressed interest in learning sign language the following semester at Arizona State University, where she was studying psychology. She knew I wasn't in school but never asked me about it, though there wasn't much to tell. I'd given community college a try after obtaining my GED, but it didn't stick.

Anyway, I went to the campus library while Madeline was in class and found a sign language chart to photocopy and cut up, then pasted together a note proclaiming how much I liked her. I slipped the note into her hand, and she gave a look before slipping into her Powerpuff Girls book bag.

A few days later her father appeared at the Arizona Biltmore for his tee time, but Madeline wasn't with him. She didn't always show, but she usually alerted me if she wasn't going to be there. I thought nothing of it until the end of the round, when her father asked me to drop by his hotel that Saturday, to talk. I was besieged by panic, which was magnified when I couldn't get a hold of Madeline for the rest of the week.

Madeline told me her parents were divorcing and that her father was living in a hotel, but the extent of the situation wasn't apparent until I was parked in the hotel lot, next to her father's vintage Corvette. The ragtop had a tear in it that I hadn't previously noticed. I once overheard him telling someone in a golf foursome that he kept a handgun in the glove box. The other members of the foursome did too, and someone cracked that most of the glove boxes in Phoenix likely had a *pistola* inside.

My emotions in the days leading up to Saturday were all over, and by the time I was behind the wheel and driving to the hotel, I was exhausted and ragged from a bout of insomnia the night before. But as I mounted the exterior steps up to Madeline's father's hotel room, I turned back and looked at the Corvette. Moments later I was at the top landing of the stairs with the handgun from the glove box tucked behind my back, under my shirt, my sweaty skin sticking to the cold metal. It was like walking with a short metal

pipe where it shouldn't be, but a powerful feeling came over me as the father's numbered door came into view. Everyone has to decide what kind of person they are, and Madeline had confided to me in the early twilight hours after Q-Fest, both of us drunk on Southern Comfort and Diet Pepsi, that her father had decided that he was the kind of person who would do things to his daughters that most would, and all should, not. She regretted saying it immediately, and I pretended not to have heard it, or to understand, and never brought it up again, though it consumed my thoughts on the golf course as her father had the nerve to joke and banter with the others in his foursome, as if he weren't a perverted scumbag. I was haunted by her confession, and the powerlessness I felt in the face of it. How could I let it slide, knowing? I pictured her father on his knees on the dirty hotel carpet, me towering over his small frame, pressing his gun into the back of his head. A fever gripped me as I approached his door. The gun was warm now from my body heat. No one knew I was meeting him, not even, presumably, Madeline. Maybe she would know it was me, maybe not. My exit strategy, if implicated, would be to ask Madeline to provide me with an alibi. Regardless of where things stood with her, I was sure she would help. My mind reeled thinking about all the terrible things the father had done to her and her sister, amplified by who knew what other horrible things he'd done in his life. He'd made his choice, had decided what kind of person he was. Long ago I'd decided too. My life had been made harder by the decision to be the kind of person who didn't look the other way, who didn't let things slide, who always said something without regard for whatever would follow. And because Jesus Christ was just a historical figure to me, nothing more, I would have to deal only with the laws of men, if that. I barely knew Madeline's father. I wasn't always his caddy. Who would put the two of us together at a hotel off the freeway? Who would believe it? Surely there were more-plausible suspects in her father's life.

I knocked on the motel door. A high-pitched shriek I recognized

filtered through the air. The door flew open and Madeline smiled at me, her father waving from the far side of the tiny motel room. An old black-and-white Christmas movie was playing on the television. I stepped from the blazing December sunlight into the cool room, which had been converted into a bachelor's apartment. Outside of the two single beds, you could easily have mistaken it for a dorm room. The gun felt like a boulder on my back, and I spent the next half hour or so worried the thing would fire when I was offered a chair to watch the last of the movie.

The Red Hot Chili Peppers were the headliners for Q-Fest, but me and Madeline hadn't heard of them. They weren't the ubiquitous Seussian rockers they are today. We just knew the one song, "Higher Ground," which the band saved as an encore, because it was on the radio. It was probably another decade or so before I realized that "Higher Ground" was a cover of a Stevie Wonder song. The Chili Peppers certainly didn't mention it that night. So many times I've been fooled by bands presenting songs as their own on the assumption that I'd know it was a cover:

Like "Red Red Wine" by UB40.

Or "Blinded by the Light" by Manfred Mann.

Or "I Love Rock 'n Roll" by Joan Jett.

Or "Tainted Love" by Soft Cell.

Or "Twist and Shout" by the Beatles.

Or "Cum on Feel the Noize" by Quiet Riot.

Or "The Tide Is High" by Blondie.

Or "It's All Over Now" and "Time Is on My Side" by the Rolling Stones.

Who sucks more than the Rolling Stones? Though in their defense, how did American radio listeners ever know they dug rhythm and blues until the Stones appropriated it and packaged it in some poses and bad acting?

I purposely left out the detail that Madeline was Hispanic. It isn't important, and you know how people start discounting what you're saying when they learn this or that extraneous detail. Her

father was not Hispanic, but her mother, whom I never met, clearly was. Madeline insisted when that she wasn't Mexican, but Hispanic. I was too dumb to know the difference and was worried that it was a subtle form of racism, but she said, "Mexicans live in Mexico, dummy," and that's all it was.

I remember the motel had a Thomas Kinkade painting on the wall, the one that looks like the sun is setting in Venice. Those paintings are a trip! You swear they are battery-operated. Ever see the ones that look like it's raining? The only artist, guaranteed, whose works are sold in shopping malls. So what? You bury them in the ground for hundreds of years and who knows what people will be saying about them in the future? How many artists hanging in fancy museums today were the laughingstocks of their age? Losers and weirdos. Reliant on the patronage of this rich person or that . Not our man Thomas Kinkade. Every fifth house you enter in Arizona proudly displays a Kinkade. He even had the good business sense to die an artistic death from booze and drugs, leaving his wife and girlfriend to fight over his estate.

That lameness about how the Arizona Biltmore Hotel tries to fool everyone into thinking it was designed by Frank Lloyd Wright, rather than one of Wright's students, is exactly like how the disciples of Christ try to put their words on Jesus.

What's funny—and funny ha-ha, not funny queer—is how Jesus and Saint Nicholas are both historical figures who, by all accounts, were kind and generous, but at some point in our lives we are told to double down on Jesus and start thinking about Saint Nicholas as a fairy tale, saddling him with magical realism involving a sleigh and reindeer. Even renaming him Santa.

Speaking of gifts: Madeline's father had asked me to meet him in his hotel room because he understood from Madeline that I was deeply in debt and was having a hard time making any headway with my life because of it, and he offered me an interest-free loan to help me get my head above water. It's true the job caddying at the Arizona Biltmore was mostly about the tips, but I secretly

also hoped to apprentice myself to one of the businessmen from the Phoenix 40, the annual list of the richest Phoenicians, to start me on an upward trajectory.

But the worst moment of my life played out in that hotel room when I accepted a check for a couple thousand dollars, Madeline beaming as her father wrote it out, me never considering not cashing it, or repaying it, the handgun cold again like a block of ice down the back of my pants.

Everyone has to decide what kind of person they're going to be.

Madeline never said anything about my note, and she never appeared again in the clubhouse while her father golfed. I quit my caddying gig a month or so after the loan was given, before the first payment was due.

John Huston's line in *Chinatown*, when he says to Jack Nicholson's character, "Most people never have to face the fact that at the right time and the right place, they're capable of *anything*," meant one thing before I met Madeline and another after. Truthfully, I could never watch that film again, but that line is in my marrow now. As someone who moved around a lot as a kid, I lost the sinuous connection to the everyday human condition that binds people together. But I know I'm not capable of anything. I spend too much time thinking about my limitations, and worrying over any lines I'd be willing to cross.

Some lines you can't know you'd cross until after you've crossed them. I was prepared to put a bullet in Madeline's father's head that day. I was. I was sure it was the right thing to do. There was a moment that afternoon when it would've been cowardly not to. That's how quickly wrong becomes right. I still carry immense shame that I didn't follow through, regardless of the circumstances. For a long time after, I fooled myself that the loan I'd accepted in place of my thirst for murder was a lateral impulse, but forever afterward the memory filled me with shame, and at some point I convinced myself that I'd never borrowed the money, or that I'd borrowed it and paid it back.

Do you sometimes wonder whatever happened to people whose paths you crossed, if briefly? The ones the internet can't help you hunt up because you don't know a last name, or never knew a name to begin with? The face of the aspiring vampire who sat on the purloined futon has faded, and I never knew her name, but what remains of her essence always invades my brain when I hear the opening of the song "Never Let Me Down Again" by Depeche Mode, from the *Music for the Masses* album. The cutting and the bloodletting began as that song blared through the expensive sound system in the apartment where I found myself, swept along as I was in a stream of concertgoers after the *Rattle and Hum* show at Sun Devil Stadium. My clearest recollection is that the apartment complex was a new stucco construction, painted pink and turquoise. And only college students lived there, giving the place a campus feel, or that of a co-ed clubhouse. I've driven the streets of Tempe searching for any glimmer of the pink and turquoise, but it's clear that the complex was either razed or painted over.

The vampires floated through my mind when my CBGB friend and I filtered into that bar on Cape Cod, the Depeche Mode blaring as if on cue. I shouldn't have said what I said to the centaur and his friends. Anyone who knows me knows I'm slow to anger, can laugh off almost anything, or offer a tasteless joke or cynical comment in an attempt to deflect the ugliness that is always lapping around the edges of every conversation, every circumstance. Never give anything power over you. But when the centaur asked us to leave, and said why, I was one foot up on the steps of Madeline's father's hotel again, the same blackness rising, and the rush of anger crested and crashed in an instant. The centaur and his friends gave a fearful look, as if their bubble had been pierced by a lethal virus. The return ferry to Boston that night was mostly empty, the boat whooshing through the darkness as it carried me back to my exile.

One of the centaur's friends was wearing a pink T-shirt with a white linen coat and pants, and espadrilles, a look popularized by Don Johnson's character Sonny Crockett on the hit television show

Miami Vice. I'd had a similar outfit and worked it into the rotation my freshman year. This was when I was living in San Diego. All the streets in my neighborhood were named for writers. The foster family I was living with, the Wallaces, lived on Sterne Street, next door to an inveterate pot smoker who owned a string of successful hat shops and who was always blaring Pavement albums on the weekends. The pot smoker razzed me from his porch on one of my Sonny Crockett days, but we would get high and watch *Miami Vice* every Friday night. He'd had a long-running dispute with the Wallaces, the nature of which I never learned, and I sometimes thought he was cultivating me as a double agent, though he never asked me about them. Maybe he just sensed a deeply unhappy freshman who, for some reason, liked to dress up like Sonny Crockett.

Legend is that the then head of NBC scribbled the note "MTV Cops" and the idea for the series was born. As legends go, it's too predictive to be taken as truth, but there wasn't anything else like it on television. The slick cars, the hit-radio songs, the fashionable clothes, the perfect interplay between Crockett and his partner, Ricardo Tubbs, played by the winsome Philip Michael Thomas. And the guest stars! Phil Collins as a con artist–cum–game show host (and Kyra Sedgwick as his accomplice), Pam Grier as Tubbs's old girlfriend, Helena Bonham Carter as Crockett's girlfriend, John Turturro as the leader of a prostitution ring, Julia Roberts as a drug dealer's girlfriend, Gene Simmons as a drug dealer, Ted Nugent as a drug dealer, Bruce Willis as an arms smuggler, Liam Neeson as an Irish terrorist, George Takei as a money launderer, Chris Cooper as a dirty cop. Eartha Kitt, Little Richard, G. Gordon Liddy, Frank Zappa, Leonard Cohen, Willie Nelson killing it as a Texas Ranger.

The show was edgy, too. One of the episodes from the first season has Crockett running into Evan, a former vice cop he came up with who is now undercover with an arms dealer. Crockett begs off the investigation that has brought him back into Evan's orbit, but no dice. Tubbs wants the backstory, but Crockett gives him an icy stare and tells him to drop it, which of course Tubbs doesn't,

instead pulling Evan's file, where Tubbs learns that Crockett and Evan went through the academy together with a third officer, Mike Orgel. Tubbs's snooping around chaps Crockett's hide, and they decide here near the end of season 1 not to be buddies, but just to do the job together and leave it at the office. As it was the show's first season, it was highly believable that this partnership might not work out. (Unless you were a television executive, I guess.) But in the inevitable scene where Crockett seeks out Tubbs and they make up, Crockett relates how the third officer, Orgel, tried to beg out of an investigation he and Crockett and Evan were on that required them to infiltrate gay bars. Evan started giving Orgel shit, saying things like, "Mike's afraid someone will recognize him ." The way dudes did in the '80s, calling each other "faggot" or "queer" and saying this or that was gay. Crockett tells Tubbs that Orgel *was* worried he would be recognized, that Orgel was indeed a homosexual, and that Orgel walked into a police situation with a shooter shortly after and was shot dead. "Suicide," Crockett says. And ever since, Evan has been volunteering for every kamikaze assignment in the hopes of meeting the same fate, such is his guilt. The anguish on Crockett's face when he tells Tubbs all of this relayed to all of us viewers that he, too, has been carrying the same guilt for forever and, by extrapolation, that it is important to always do the right thing, to stand up for someone else's rights and beliefs, regardless of whether or not you share the same rights and beliefs.

It was a powerful television moment. And it flushed to the forefront of my mind when the centaur asked me and my CBGB friend to leave the bar on Cape Cod. And even though I shouldn't have said it, the words "You're no better than those who hate gay people" left my lips before I could check them. The disservice done to whatever suffering he and his friends had had in their lives as homosexuals had been delivered. Some things when spoken become tattoos, and mine has been an indelible part of me since that night.

When I was living in Florida in the early 1990s, there was a buzz one day that Magic Johnson was going to make an announcement,

and in the pre-internet days there wasn't much more information than that until, at a seemingly hastily arranged press conference, the Laker point guard announced he was HIV positive and would immediately be retiring from basketball. The next night he was a guest on his friend Arsenio Hall's talk show, where the pair talked expansively about Magic's new life and his role as a spokesman about the virus, especially within the black community, where HIV was spreading at an alarming rate. We had the television on in the bar where I was bartending, and there was an odd moment where the idea that HIV was strictly a gay disease was dismissed and Magic said something like, "I'm as heterosexual as they get," and the crowd whooped and hollered their affirmation and appreciate for the fact, as if the average person were so invested in the sexual preferences of one Earvin "Magic" Johnson. But you knew you were witnessing an important television moment, and—unlike the fiction of *Miami Vice* but just as powerful—all of us watching could sense that there'd been another shift in our understanding of the world at large, and how important it was to be inclusive rather than reductive.

How many people believe John F. Kennedy was a progressive threat to the Establishment because of the Oliver Stone movie? Not sure the history books bear that out, but they don't bear out much of what's in the film. Too much of history is too boring to craft compelling cinema from. But it wasn't until many years later that I learned that the whole enterprise was essentially factless. The tip-off should've been that even with all that compelling evidence— the testimony of the characters brilliantly played by Joe Pesci, the aspiring priest who ended up a CIA mercenary and confesses to his role before being murdered; Kevin Bacon, the young homosexual who was the object of the affections of Clay Shaw, played by Tommy Lee Jones, who may or may not have been in the CIA, and witnessed many of the characters plotting Kennedy's assassination; and Donald Sutherland as a nameless government official who breathlessly reels off a tight narrative of the entire conspiracy and how high it went—the trial ended in a not-guilty verdict. Others

have been convicted on less. And then the crazy magic bullet theory, with its impossible ballistic logic.

Joe Pesci's portrayal of David Ferrie was Oscar-worthy, and Ferrie's paranoid ambivalence before confession felt so emotionally true that you as the viewer needed Kevin Costner as Jim Garrison, the New Orleans district attorney who charged Clay Shaw with the conspiracy, to come through. But then it turns out that in real life David Ferrie always said he was innocent, that he didn't know anything about anything, and that Pesci's amazing performance was just a trick. Imagine if Ferrie had still been alive (he actually died of natural causes and wasn't murdered) when the film was made. Oliver Stone would've had to buy his silence, or pay libel.

And the conspiracy narrative Sutherland spools? It's taken directly from what *The Guinness Book of Records* considers the Most Famous Literary Hoax, the book *The Report from Iron Mountain*, which was cheekily published as nonfiction but was always fiction, like the magic bullet theory, which isn't really built on the laws of physics or any other science. The reverse of what the film suggests about the movement of Kennedy's head has been proven in scientific re-creations, which confirm the same in the Warren Commission report.

What's remarkable about the movie, though, is not that my generation believed its presentation as a near documentary, but that so many who grew up in the Kennedy era believed it too. You could charge Oliver Stone with gross insensitivity for exploiting the unhealed wounds of those who had to live through that and other assassinations of the '60s. Viewed strictly as a piece of art, the movie has a conspiratorial, antigovernment vibe that feels historically accurate, and you can hear its echoes in conversations with baby boomers, who essentially mistrust the Written Record, or What Is Told. Their children, by comparison—my generation—simply don't care if it's true or not. Our parents' paranoia bred our indifference.

Which likely accounts for the dearth of Generation X politicians. Another trial that seemed like a slam dunk, though lacking in

cinematic style, was the murder trial of O. J. Simpson. The case had Hollywood elements—a former football star–turned–actor, beautiful victims, outraged family members demanding justice, all the defense lawyers money could buy, and the same judge who had previously put Phoenix financier Charlie Keating in custody—but all the acting was terrible, and save for the twist ending, it might've gone relatively unreviewed. The trial confirmed a few widely held suspicions, paramount among them the idea that the rich and famous are not necessarily as intelligent as or smarter than the rest of us. That their privileged lives shelter them from real-world consequences we all would face if we behaved similarly. Or didn't have the money to maneuver around egregious mistakes.

But rich and famous or not, murder is a heinous and serious crime, and so we all watched, riveted to our television screens as the so-called trial of the century played out episodically. The mistake most of us who were surprised by the verdict made was that we believed the jurors were telling us that O.J. didn't commit the murders. That was a head-scratcher in view of the evidence and the slim mathematical probability that anyone else might've done it. It would be a long while before we heard what the jury was trying to say about racial injustice in general and racial injustice specifically at the hands of the Los Angeles police. The verdict as a form of protest would come to make sense down the road, and everyone would have to settle for themselves if freeing O.J. was the right bargain.

A by-product of the Simpson trial was that finally the line between fame and infamy had been crossed forever. Previously, infamy had been the last-place prize for those who had aspirations of becoming famous but who had reached for the brass ring and felt their fingertips brush it on the way down. Or those who had never even sniffed the brass ring. For example, you might think that appearing on the world stage as a college dropout who fit the description of a surfer frat boy right out of central casting might expose you to ridicule, as it did Kato Kaelin, the witness who'd lived in O.J.'s guest house and heard a thump against his wall on

the night in question. And you might think, previously, that you'd spend the rest of your life trying to undo that image of yourself, to no avail. Once Kato the aspiring but ultimately failed actor, always the aspiring but failed actor. You might expect that appearing at a local car show, or in a spoofy national commercial during the Super Bowl, might be the best someone like Kato Kaelin could dream of after the lampooning he took in the media. And, previously, you would've been correct. But Kato Kaelin was able to parlay his appearance as a witness for the prosecution, and not really one of their main witnesses, into a long television career. It must've been strange to move effortlessly into a Hollywood orbit larger than the one O.J. could provide him. It was a remarkable rise even for the fickle demarcations in Tinseltown. Whether or not his television career was based solely on his trial personality is not for me to say. Hollywood does love to typecast.

Or is it that we the audience require typecasting? They say the mark of genius is the ability to hold two opposing ideas in your mind at the same time. But we're not a society of geniuses, by the strict definition, so is Hollywood just reacting to the reality they've been given, as tabloid newspapers always claim? And, more disturbingly, are we faux-outraged at the concept but secretly relieved by it?

Are we generally satisfied with Orville Redenbacher as the folksy spokesperson for a beloved brand of popcorn, or can we also admit that he was a pioneer who made an important contribution to agriculture by creating the strain of popcorn that served as the foundation for his empire?

How did the rest of the United States House of Representatives treat Gopher from *The Love Boat* and Cooter from *The Dukes of Hazzard* when the actors were elected to their hallowed ranks?

So many times a beloved actor in a celebrated TV series has a hard time convincing the public that he or she isn't the character we've come to love. Don Johnson was able to shed Sonny Crockett to become Nash Bridges, as well as a handful of believable film roles. Or maybe we were always thinking, *That's Sonny Crockett.*

Was Ted Danson believable as Dr. John Becker for those 129 episodes, or were we thinking, *That's Sam Malone playing a doctor in the Bronx?* Same for Julia Louis-Dreyfus—Elaine from *Seinfeld*, my generation's *I Love Lucy*—in *The New Adventures of the Old Christine?* The geniuses among us would allow for both, I suppose.

We forever want Molly Ringwald to be the girl from the John Hughes movies; we don't even care which one. We just want her to remain America's sweetheart. Never mind her subsequent career in film or her endeavors as a writer. It makes it a lot harder to take the "Which John Hughes Character Are You?" quiz after we've had a few too many.

What's fascinating about the painter Thomas Kinkade is how vehement his detractors and critics were. The arguments proffered for his artistic illegitimacy were many but hardly cohesive. He sold his paintings on QVC. He didn't actually paint the paintings. The so-called Kinkade glow in every painting was a gimmick. He only painted similarly styled cottages and landscapes. His paintings sold not in art galleries, but in shopping malls.

It's a sure bet that those who turned up their noses at Kinkade are fans of the film *Magnolia*.

It wasn't that long ago that another artist commercially produced his art, conceiving of the original idea and having apprentices complete the finished product. And instead of glowing paintings, his gimmick was to create meaningless art out of the meaningless products of everyday lives. Soup cans, celebrity portraits, boxes of Brillo pads. When asked what the work represented, Andy Warhol shied away from answers, which enhanced his pop star aura. We're all old enough to know that the level of fame Warhol achieved required cunning, and silence. A mystery is preferable to all else.

Warhol collectors, *Magnolia* fans all, wouldn't see or acknowledge their kinship with Kinkade fans, but both admire technical mastery and gimmickery.

And by rights, both would be fans of the original commercial artist, Albrecht Dürer, whose mass-produced engravings made him

wealthier than any of his contemporaries, who likely were in the service of their patrons. (Learned that from Rick Steves.)

The unspoken, sometimes spoken, central objection to Kinkade's work was that the fervently religious saw God in his paintings, and their religiosity was the basis for Kinkade's popularity. And while it might be okay for tourists to flock to museums around the world to gawk at paintings from centuries past that either depict religion outright or seek to express a belief in God, it's not okay for your grandparents to fight traffic and shuffle through the food court on their way to find the paintings that soothe and comfort them.

Many of the shopping malls on the west side of Phoenix, the older section of the city, as well as in the suburb of Mesa, populated mostly by Mormons, had Kinkade dealers. Not so the malls in the richer suburbs, such as Scottsdale or Paradise Valley. Or, of course, Tempe, the college town.

Before upscale malls were developed in Scottsdale, the toniest shopping center in Phoenix was Biltmore Fashion Park, built along Camelback Road, dubbed the Camelback Corridor, so named for being in the shadow of Camelback Mountain, a nearby geological red rock wonder in the shape of a camel. Biltmore Fashion Park abutted the aforementioned Arizona Biltmore Hotel, giving the outdoor shopping center a proximity to luxury.

Across Camelback Road from Biltmore Fashion Park in the 1980s and 1990s was a complex of buildings known as American Continental Corporation, the headquarters of financier Charles H. Keating Jr. Before Charlie Keating came to symbolize the naked greed of the time, he was a pioneering antipornography crusader appointed to an antiobscenity commission by President Richard Nixon. When the commission confirmed in its report that pornography did not corrupt morals and lead to an escalation in crime, Charlie was the lone dissenter. The Nixon administration gave Charlie help with writing a rebuttal in the form of speechwriter Pat Buchanan. However, the rebuttal was widely mocked by both political parties. Undaunted, Charlie took the experience back home

to Cincinnati, where he waged war against filthy movies, filthy plays, and hotel chains that featured filthy in-room programming. He even produced his own documentary about the dangers of perversion.

One of the clients at the law firm where Charlie worked was a financial services holding company, American Financial. Charlie ended up leaving his legal career to become an executive at American Financial, and over the years he was the cleaner, whose job it was to fire employees of the companies that American Financial acquired. But soon there was an SEC investigation, and Charlie was charged with filing false reports and defrauding investors. Charlie resigned from American Financial, and the same year he turned up in Arizona, ready for reinvention.

Phoenix was a small city then, ripe for the kind of real estate expansion Charlie envisioned. It wasn't long before American Continental was the biggest home builder in the valley. Soon after, Charlie bought Lincoln Savings and Loan, a California bank whose conservative investments made it a perennial loser, though a safe bet for its customers. The federal government deregulated the savings and loan industry, meaning S and Ls could use their deposits for riskier financial projects, and soon Lincoln's profits increased fivefold. But the government quickly realized the downside of said investments, namely that they exposed the government's guarantee to depositors to potentially crippling risks. So the savings and loans were reregulated and ordered to reduce their risky holdings.

But Charlie said, "I don't think so," and went to war with the government. He enlisted a handful of United States senators, known colloquially as the Keating Five, to plead his case with the government. At a hastily organized press conference at the Arizona Biltmore Hotel, Charlie was famously asked if he expected a return on his investment of campaign donations to the senators, and he said, "I certainly hope so."

But it didn't work out, and Charlie was indicted and ultimately convicted and sent to prison, his company liquidated by the

government. The Phoenician, a luxury hotel he built in the side of Camelback Mountain with marble imported from Italy, among other lavish touches, was sold to a group of Kuwaitis for twenty-five cents on the dollar and still stands as a monument to Charlie's opulent lifestyle. Near the entrance of the Phoenician is the Jokake Inn, the facade of which was used as the home of the fictional Nathan Arizona in the film *Raising Arizona*.

There are a number of terrible Nicolas Cage movies, but he's made so many that it's just the law of averages that some are mediocre or not great. But the breadth of roles Cage has played over the years puts him in the never-boring and almost-always-surprising category. Everyone likes risk takers—we cheer when they win, and deride them for trying when they don't, but they don't go unnoticed by us.

My first stint in New York City, in the late 1990s, gave a glimpse of what it would be like to live among an entire city of risk takers. The top whatever percent of ambitious people from all the hometowns across the globe seemed to have found their way to New York. I was only chasing a girl I'd met in Arizona, still an ambition, but a low-level one by comparison. My first couple of days in New York, I wandered Manhattan, unsure of how the subway system worked and feeling a little exposed as I ebbed and flowed with the throngs of people mobbing up and down the island. Back in Phoenix, you'd see everything through your windshield. Drive to where you were going, see the place, get in your car and drive back. But the ribbons of pavement in New York brought me into the mix.

I found myself in Lenox Hill, on the Upper East Side, along with a constant crowd of onlookers at the "grave site" of an illusionist who had buried himself in a plastic see-through coffin as a feat of endurance. Another see-through box filled with water was placed on top of the coffin, and I wondered what we all looked like to the illusionist peering up through the water. People waved and took pictures. Someone said that the stunt was a tribute to Harry Houdini, who was an idol of the illusionist's and who'd had plans

for a similar stunt but died before he could perform it.

I also stood at the makeshift memorial of flowers and messages in front of the building in Tribeca where John F. Kennedy Jr. had lived with his wife. Kennedy and his wife and sister-in-law had been on their way to a wedding of another Kennedy on Martha's Vineyard in a plane piloted by JFK Jr. when the plane went down short of the Vineyard. A Coast Guard search finally turned up the plane and its passengers in the cold waters, and everyone's hearts broke for the handsome son of the assassinated president and his beautiful wife and sister-in-law. We get spooked when tragedy befalls those who lead quote-unquote charmed lives. It confirms our vulnerability, that we're out here on our own, without advantage of wealth or pedigree, and that more likely than not, we won't escape tragedy. Dying in your sleep of old age is mostly a myth.

The near-universal acclaim for *Raising Arizona* was a welcome surprise to those of us toiling in the desert heat. Especially given that the state had turned into a punch line since Evan Mecham, the Mormon used-car salesman who had become governor, was an undisciplined, uneducated racist. Blacks weren't the only object of his prejudice: he told a Jewish delegation that America was a Christian nation, and relayed to a local Kiwanis club how on a recent trip to Japan he gave a golf club as a present to the head of a prominent bank and how the banker "got round eyes" when Mecham told him how many golf courses Arizona boasted. And then, of course, he said on the television program *60 Minutes* that homosexuality was illegal and that he wasn't prejudiced against gays, just that their lifestyle broke the law, a line his supporters relied heavily on when defending him. But like all things, to not see it is to not want to see it.

A recall of Mecham was initiated on the 181st day of his administration, the earliest date as prescribed by law , and it didn't take long to collect the signatures needed. Shortly after Bono and U2 left town, a recall election was scheduled. Mecham decried the "homosexuals and dissident Democrats" trying to turn him out of office, but the special election set to recall the governor never took

place, as Mecham was convicted on an obstruction of justice charge related to one of his aides making death threats against a witness for various investigations into Mecham, as well as "high crimes, misdemeanors or malfeasance" for diverting state money in the form of a loan to one of his Pontiac dealerships. Upon conviction by the Arizona State Senate, Mecham was removed and the secretary of state, Rose Mofford, whose beehive hairdo was legendary around the state capitol, became the first female governor of Arizona, presaging a time two decades later when every elected high office in the state would be held by women.

So it was fun to see Phoenix and the surroundings up on the big screen. Though there were plenty who thought maybe the joke was on Phoenicians, and because of the national headlines about the Mecham saga, politicians worried that the film was more oxygen for the bonfire consuming the state's reputation. In the wake of the Mecham antics, there was a boycott of the state by Stevie Wonder, the rap group Public Enemy released a protest song called "By the Time I Get to Arizona," and the NFL withdrew the honor of Phoenix's being a host site of an upcoming Super Bowl. The Super Bowl situation dragged on for more than half a decade, until voters finally passed a paid Martin Luther King Jr. holiday, mostly, some felt, to win back the right to host the Super Bowl and reap the economic windfall. Arizona was indeed the site of Super Bowl XXX; or rather Tempe, as the game was played at Sun Devil Stadium, since Arizona didn't have a professional football stadium then. Plans for the Cardinals to have their own stadium had to be shelved for nearly two decades, owing to the financial upheaval of the savings and loan crisis.

Still, how cool is it to see something familiar in a movie? Not just Sun Devil Stadium in the football game scene at the end of *Raising Arizona*, but Lost Dutchman State Park in Apache Junction, where H.I. gets into a fight at a family picnic, and the gas station on Deer Valley Road where he famously steals the Huggies. Every time after, whenever you'd pass near any of the filming locations, you'd get a jolt

that Hollywood actors knew where you lived, had seen what you'd seen, and you were dying to know what they thought of everything that was swirling in the background of their minstrel show. Maybe that sounds silly, but it's akin to when someone is suffering with a diagnosis and a celebrated person announces to the world that he or she is similarly diagnosed . Magic Johnson's announcement that he was HIV positive made a tremendous difference not just in how the virus was perceived, but in how people who had contracted the virus were regarded. When the actor Mandy Patinkin tells the world that he had to have a double corneal transplant, it makes the procedure a little less scary for the person who needs the same and whose friends have never even heard of such a thing. Even if the celebrated person is forced into confession before being exposed by the vile tabloid press, the calming effect is the same. For a moment we get amnesia about the socioeconomic differences that might dictate the variable quality of treatment and just revel in the connection. Suffering anonymously feels so ignoble and lonely.

New York City is the ultimate movie set, and you can't help but think of all the films you've seen that have New York as a backdrop when you visit or live there. The skylines in *On the Waterfront*. Fifth Avenue in *Breakfast at Tiffany's*. Before the Dakota on Central Park West was known for the terrible murder of John Lennon, it was the backdrop for the couple in *Rosemary's Baby*. Gene Hackman's wild pursuit along the D train through Bensonhurst in *The French Connection* reveals the chaotic madness of New York maybe better than any thing else. *Saturday Night Fever's* John Travolta trucks into the city from Bay Ridge to reinvent himself, but a thousand Travoltas materialize on the streets of Manhattan after dark. The Broadway of *All That Jazz*. The East Village of *Desperately Seeking Susan*. Spike Lee's Brooklyn in *Do the Right Thing*. The New York of all of Martin Scorsese's movies is alive both then and now. Who can blame Charlie Sheen's intoxication with the wealthy as he inhabits enclaves like 21 Club and Tavern on the Green in *Wall Street*? Glenn Close on the Upper West Side in *Fatal Attraction* is maybe

less frightening than the spoiled brats on the Upper East Side in *Metropolitan*. And, of course, the iconic scene with Meg Ryan and Billy Crystal in *When Harry Met Sally* has tourists in line at Katz's Deli at all hours.

When I finally made my way back to New York, leaving Phoenix for good, the city was constantly reminding me of the Scorsese cult film *After Hours*, a black comedy about a character played by Griffin Dunne trying to find his way home. I'd crashed out of my job as a columnist in Phoenix, and New York was an unscratched itch. One hot and sticky night in August as I packed up the meager belongings in my one-bedroom apartment in Phoenix, I e-mailed the girlfriend who had led me to New York, a British woman named Olivia, and the cosmos aligned when she e-mailed back to say that she would meet me in New York if that was the plan. I assured her it was, and there was suddenly a sense of urgency and logic to my moving east.

Olivia kept her word, though it was a bit of a cheat, as she had business in New York in her capacity as a purchasing agent for a London pharmaceutical company. So what if I was flying thousands of miles to see her, and she was making a transatlantic journey *both* for me and for business? At least I was in the mix, which was more than I had going in Phoenix. But the reunion was marred by the fact that we were complete strangers all these years later, which we discovered over drinks and dinner in the East Village. Whatever passion had fueled our romance almost a decade previous was a mystery to us as we droned on at dinner about our respective lives, our jobs, the subtext being how we both were still searching for life answers but that we were essentially strangers to each other.

After Olivia caught her flight back to London, I was left roaming the streets of New York. I'd seen *After Hours* at the Valley Art cinema back in Tempe during a film festival celebrating cult films of the 1980s, and while I'd dug it, the landscape had seemed completely foreign. But suddenly I was trudging similar New York streets, unmoored, desperate to get back to my temporary home, a room built of four walls in the middle of an artist's loft in Soho. The

desperate need to find his way home is the brilliant suspense of *After Hours*, but in my case it was less a sense of urgency than a foregone conclusion. The artist's loft was teeming with people at all hours, and even within the confines of my four walls there was never any peace. I'd come to live in the loft only as a matter of convenient rent, but there had been obvious trade-offs on the first night, when the artist invited the acrobats in a traveling circus to stay with us for the week they were in town to perform.

The first few months back in New York, wandering the streets and watching my savings decline, I worried that there was nowhere left for me to run. That I was able to hang in for a couple of years, long enough to meet the woman who would become my wife— in the other room of our Chelsea apartment now, winnowing our possessions to the essentials for our move to the Hudson River valley, close enough to visit the city anytime we'd like—redefines "miraculous." I can't say how I hung in. That's how it is for the underclass in New York. One day at a time, like an alcoholic seeking redemption. And I almost refused the invitation to the garden party at the brownstone in Brooklyn where Vanessa and I met. I remember that week had ended on a particularly down note, with my being fired from a temporary position as a researcher in a bankruptcy law firm in Midtown. It was my plan to grab a Styrofoam container of General Tso's chicken from the corner place near my apartment on the south side of Williamsburg and gorge on the salty-sweet flesh and rice, but before the fluorescent lighting of the Chinese joint could pull me in, I bumped into the guy I'd interviewed with at *The Wall Street Journal* when I thought about continuing my career as a journalist, not fully appreciating how burned my bridges were. His name escaped me, and I accepted his invitation to the party as a courtesy, planning to duck out at first chance, but not before I could overhear someone mentioning his name, which no one ever did. Had I left fifteen minutes earlier, I would've missed meeting Vanessa, a recent graduate of the School of Visual Arts who was as unmoored as I was. My empty stomach was baying, but I kept

as still as I could as I peppered Vanessa with questions about her mixed-media art, stretching the limits of my knowledge of her world before telling her how tremendous it was to meet her, hoping that we would see each other again. "How about now?" she said, and it wasn't long before I moved out of my Williamsburg apartment and into her rent-controlled one-bedroom in Greenwich Village.

It was a nerve-racking few months for me, as it had been a long time since I'd courted a love interest. Olivia a decade earlier, and before that, what? High school? But New York was an easy place to be in love, and we ate in cheap restaurants, drank watered-down well drinks in dive bars, scored discount tickets to Broadway shows, and spent a lot of time in Central Park. I was anxious about relating too much of my chaotic past and tried to dole out my story anecdotally, but the pieces shot randomly from a cannon began to seem . . . unbelievable. A nd one night, late, after we'd smoked more than a few joints in the roof garden of her apartment building, I tried to tell it chronologically, and while the end result was still a patchwork quilt, Vanessa peered at me across the darkness, a look of not just comprehension but understanding on her perfect face, and I never needed to say another word about it. Her own upbringing, in Ohio, had been as stable as growing up in Ohio sounds to outsiders. She had very few complaints. Her parents had owned a stationery store, where she'd work in the summers to make extra money. Her job at a bookstore near Grand Central Station was as much about the stationery they sold as it was about the employee discount on books.

Vanessa thought I was kidding when I told her that I'd published a novel. There was an awkward moment where, when I said I'd *written* a novel, she thought I'd come to New York to find an agent and a publisher. But I assured her that I'd moved to the city with no such ambition, or any ambition really. To prove to myself that I didn't care what I did for money, I took the test at a temp agency, dumbed down my past experience, and happily went wherever they sent me. Working nights in the print shop of a well-known cancer hospital in Midtown. Writing catalog copy for a tool company in

Brooklyn. Mostly proofreading legal briefs at law firms all over Manhattan and sometimes in New Jersey. In each place I was just an anonymous face, a passing curiosity.

The temp agency sent me to the offices of a free weekly alternative newspaper, and by chance one of the editors had just read my novel and recognized me from my author photo. He offered me a job as a book reviewer. That gig was even easier than being a temp, and the salary and benefits were welcome, but I grew to hate the assigned books on sight, and right when I was contemplating quitting, the editor who had hired me called me into his office with a hangdog expression and announced that the Arts section was being shuttered in favor of paid advertising and would I accept a buyout? I pretended to be as bummed about the change as he was, deposited their check, and celebrated my good fortune at a string of bars on my way home.

Vanessa ordered a copy of my novel, and it was a bit of a thrill to see it in her bag. She prodded me about what was true and what was fiction, and I just shrugged. "After a while you can't really tell anymore," I said. She encouraged me to write another book, but what I couldn't say was that I didn't have the key weapon all writers need in their arsenal: the ability to see all sides of everything at once. That's not just the ability to hold two opposing ideas in your mind. It's something else entirely. My former training as a newspaper columnist had encouraged me to choose a point of view and run with it.

Jimmy Stewart's apartment complex in Hitchcock's *Rear Window* was meant to be Greenwich Village. On one of my wanderings I found myself traipsing along Christopher Street near the building that was the model for the movie apartments. A film crew was set up in front of a couple of Federal-style brownstones, and I could hear the talking head saying something about how Hitchcock had had the courtyard the buildings shared photographed in all manner of weather and light in order to re-create it back in Hollywood. "Jimmy Stewart would've never made it up these stairs," the talking head laughed as the camera panned to one of the building entrances.

The most satisfying and least aggravating Hitchcock films are the ones that have the feel of a stage play—*Rear Window*, *Rope*, and *Dial M for Murder*, the latter two of which were actually based on stage plays. What Hitchcock gets right, always, is a character's obsessive nature. In *Rope* and *Dial M*, the murderers have considered every detail and are consequently quick on their feet when variables challenge their version of events. *Rope* features the added stress of the murder dredging up a bitter fracture between the two murderers, which their onetime teacher (Jimmy Stewart again!) senses, leading him to deduce what has really happened. The Jimmy Stewart in *Rear Window* similarly pieces together a murder, though the exercise is not as existential as it is in *Rope*.

Phoenix features in the opening sequence of *Psycho*. After the credits dissolve, you can see Camelback Mountain in the distance as the camera shows the skyline. A nifty camera pan brings into focus the original downtown, much of which still exists: the Hotel San Carlos; the Adams Hotel; the Jefferson Hotel, where Janet Leigh and her boyfriend are holed up. The building with the giant antenna remains, though the antenna does not. A different antenna exists in the same general area and is often confused for the one in *Psycho*.

It seems like utter nonsense that *Psycho* is not named as Hitchcock's best film, over the likes of *Vertigo*. Perhaps the inherent snobbery of the Magnolias against horror films is to blame. But there's little doubt that the DNA of *Psycho* is in every subsequent horror movie, especially slasher flicks. The shot-for-shot remake of the film by Gus Van Sant, though a terrible failure, was terrifically successful at pointing up just how revolutionary Hitchcock's version was in its time. Cinemagoers in 1960 were rightly shocked, and possibly understood that the stifling culture they lived in was being criticized in the bargain. By the time the Van Sant version arrived almost four decades later, the audience was neither shocked, nor sympathetic to the culture being critiqued. Instead the film is more revealing as a meta exercise in recycled content. Everything comes from something, but the remade *Psycho* proves that the pivot away

from the original source material is key to a successful homage.

Hitchcock forbade cinemas from allowing late seating at *Psycho* showings, which you can appreciate if you've ever suffered through shadowy figures filtering in long after a movie has started. It's unreal that in the old days of cinema, patrons were allowed to join a movie in progress, allowed to watch until the end and then stay for whatever they might've missed from the beginning. But Hitchcock was insistent that the beginning, middle, and end were paramount to the full thrill of *Psycho*, and he undertook a campaign to convince theater owners, who largely abided by the novelty.

Ever hear this little chestnut: "Who are you to judge?" You know whose favorite refrain that is? Selfish people's. It's the ultimate cover story.

But there are some easy calls. You don't have to be pure of heart to point out that the drowning of untended children in swimming pools every year is the result of bad parenting. Or that drunk driving is a careless, selfish act. Same for animal cruelty. You can probably judge O.J. Simpson's guilt or innocence pretty easily. There's a low-level current of everyday selfishness that has become so commonplace that while we might get angry at the driver who cuts us off in traffic, we've been told so many times not to cast the first stone that we can't admit the obvious to ourselves: that driver is a selfish person and, by extension, a terrible citizen. What's good for them is good for them. Who cares about *you*? Perhaps it's nostalgic to think there was once a time when people weren't so blatantly selfish, when we might go out of our way to disguise our worse impulses. We're forever telling children that it's okay to make mistakes, which it is, but when mistakes are habitual, they cease being mistakes and become conduct. A lot of violence has been done in the service of religion, but the saying "Let he who is without sin cast the first stone ," derived from the Bible verse, has done as much or more damage as any other biblical passage, as it lets us all off the hook. We're no longer held accountable, except by the laws of man. (And, of course, God, if you like.)

You're thinking it, so I'll say it: a further problem, unpopular to even think, forget about uttering aloud, is that not all people are created equal. That might sound like a Magnolian thing to say, but it's just a factual statement and not an emotional one based on race, religion, money, or social status, so it's not an excuse for discrimination. The root cause of this inequality depends on where you land on the nature-versus-nurture argument.

Plus, all those commonsense product warnings and disclaimers belie the unspoken truth. "Once used rectally, the thermometer should not be used orally." Or: "Never iron clothes while being worn." You might think that's just lawyers being lawyers, but if a base doesn't need covering, the players on the field will hold their positions.

There are some disadvantages in life so extreme that it's not fair to judge that person against someone who hasn't suffered similarly, but what about the person who has not only overcome those disadvantages, but has been so assiduous with the handling of his or her own life that he or she has excelled? Exception to the rule, or a poor reflection on the person who didn't excel? Can we have an opinion about that?

Even if we admit that people have complex inner lives, and that their own personal web of experiences and emotions influences their decision-making, does that ever allow people to behave selfishly and not for the greater good? Did the person with the complicated life story who repeatedly [insert selfish act here] just make a mistake? Or is it okay to call out his or her behavior?

O. J. Simpson?

Roman Polanski?

Frank Lloyd Wright?

Charlie Keating?

Easier if we just fit them for a black hat and move on with our lives.

In truth, we spend a lot of energy judging one another, subconsciously but also consciously. But in both cases silently, either

out of fear that a society that openly judges itself will live under a depressive cloud of paranoia, or out of a sense of superiority. And so we make little judgments only to ourselves, casting stones left and right, all the time, but claiming the opposite in polite conversation, insinuating that we all of us live in glass houses.

Related: turning the other cheek. For the same reasons re lack of accountability. Don't get me started.

Before Olivia caught her flight back to London, she mentioned that her old friend Shelleyan was living the high life in New York. Olivia called Shelleyan "our mutual friend," but Shelleyan was exclusively Olivia's friend from our days at Glendale Community College back in Phoenix. I've never settled with myself whether Olivia was oblivious to Shelleyan's taunts directed toward yours truly, or if she just looked the other way. At the time I was so desperate for Olivia's affections that either was acceptable to me, but sitting across the table from her in the well-lit and decidedly unromantic restaurant Olivia had chosen as the site of our reunion, the former seemed impossible and the latter seemed like a benign cruelty.

I actually knew Shelleyan was living in New York, as I'd bumped into her on my first go-around. I had avoided her then and was surprised when Olivia brought her up again. I could sense in Olivia's casual tone that she was fishing to see if I was somehow in touch with Shelleyan, and I imagined, perhaps spitefully, that Olivia had tried to reach out to Shelleyan but to no avail. That Shelleyan was quote-unquote living the high life in New York was a burning curiosity, but the old buried bitterness sprang from deep within me and I couldn't bring myself even to raise an eyebrow, or to hear Olivia's speculations on what it all meant.

Olivia made her life in London sound terrific, and who knows, perhaps it was. I remembered a time early on in our relationship when she confessed to me that the worst thing that could happen to her was that she'd end up back in London, living close enough to all her relatives to see them at holidays and birthday celebrations,

working a job she marginally cared about to meet her monthly obligations, punctuated by the occasional nights out with friends. She'd flung herself halfway across the globe in an effort to exorcise those demons. A problem with her visa flung her back, but she swore she'd return to Arizona once it was all straightened out. But she didn't. Now I charitably hoped that she'd forgotten about those early ambitions of flight. But who ever does? Shelleyan had gotten out, and the case could even be made that I had too, though it was my second attempt, and at that point things were going about as well as my first effort. Olivia showed me one last kindness by not asking me too much about my new life in New York. The sheer wonder and excitement of the limitless possibilities someone feels when they move to a new place is absent upon a second try at the same move, and I wouldn't have had it in me to invent a narrative plausible enough to be believed.

What's remarkable about past cinemagoers wandering into a film whenever, and watching until the story was complete, is their willingness to piece together what was being told, rather than demanding the beginning come before the middle, or the middle before the ending. Some must've stumbled upon a film's conclusion and wondered what it was all about until the opening credits appeared. The most remarkable part, though, is how that sort of in-medias-res approach is truer to life than the artifice of beginning, middle, and end, if only because, absent death, how can any of us know when we're being presented with the beginning or the middle or the end of something? We mark our birthdays, sure, and we're told that the X years are for this, and we can expect these things in the Y years, but that's just another artifice. If we're lucky enough to reach old age, we can look through the lens of retrospect and understand certain things that happened, and why, though perhaps too late to learn anything from the retrospection. But a remnant of Hitchcock's legacy has to be shaping our narrative expectations, which I'd argue has created a sense of incompleteness in our lives as we intuitively clamor to know where we are inside our own stories.

You could say we're all in the middle, all the time, but that's of no use as we try to make sense of the world around us.

Crime stories offer us the narrative structure we've been conditioned to favor. There's a comfort in learning the events leading up to a crime and then following the investigation that reveals, hopefully with satisfying twists and turns, who committed the crime and why, as well as the guilty party's requisite punishment. Unsolved mysteries like, say, the Kennedy assassination, challenge and delay the dopamine rush we experience with the arc of crime stories, so we invent conspiracy theories as the potential endings we're being denied. Less satisfying, sure, but still made to conform to our expectations.

A funny crime story with a predictable outcome in Arizona involved state legislators who got caught up in a sting operation called AzScam, named after the FBI sting Abscam a decade or so before. The plot of AzScam starred a thrice-convicted felon and purported midlevel mafioso, a handful of lobbyists, and about a tenth of the Arizona legislature. The felon posed as a lobbyist wanting to legalize gambling in the state and began meeting with and bribing legislators over the issue, all while a hidden camera was rolling. As painful as it was, Arizonans saw how easily their elected representatives could be bought, and the sting exposed the lawmakers as small, petty, and ultimately selfish people interested in improving their own lot at the expense of their position. Of course, the jig was up, and of course the nightly news had a wealth of footage to show for weeks and months leading up to the trials. Clever extrapolators opined in the national news that AzScam would shake what little faith cynical voters had in their electoral process, which would threaten to dramatically reduce the voting rolls when it might matter most. But Arizonans had been made electorally cynical by the national elections of years past, mostly when the Big Three news networks would project winners before most Arizonans could leave work to vote. Somewhere along the line that was all smoothed out, but it was then forgotten with the 2004

election, when, for the first time, modern voters were confronted with the truth that the definition of a winning candidate was not the one with the most votes, but instead the one who used a map of the United States as a game board, plotting out the states that mattered most in the quest to win the electoral college. In the aftermath of the 2004 election, a powerful essay called "Why It's Okay Not to Vote ," written anonymously, began to circulate on the burgeoning World Wide Web, though its popularity was sustained mostly by photocopying.

My first week back in New York, I happened to be passing the Whitney Museum of American Art on one of their free admission days. It was early and there weren't too many takers yet, so I sauntered into the imposing building and wandered into a room celebrating photocopier art by artists who had formed a collective called the International Society of Copier Artists. You think you have a handle on just about everything, and then you see something that you wouldn't have dreamed existed, and it takes you aback. Someone thought to use the enlarge and reduce buttons on a photocopier, as well as the dark and light functions, to create art. A lot of someones. Wild stuff, too! Cut-and-paste seemed to be another tool in the photocopier artist's arsenal too , along with a whole host of ingenious ways to manipulate images. An image's replication seemed to be at the heart of a lot of the pieces, the idea that a copy of a copy of a copy of a copy could suddenly become an original of its own.

I took in the rest of the museum that day, but my mind kept wandering back to the photocopy art, the brilliance of it. And the democratic nature of being a photocopy artist. While not everyone could afford a photocopier of their own back when they first appeared, anyone could gain access to one. No expensive studios to rent, or oils and canvases and all other manner of art supplies to buy. Any demographic was welcome to step up and give it a try. No cumbersome patronage required. I imagined several photocopier artists staying late in the offices where they slaved to pay their bills

by day, the office turning into an idea factory at night, the floor strewn with drafts in search of a finished artistic expression.

Why do you think it is that it's okay to commission a painting, or for filmmakers to fund their own movies, or for bands to underwrite the production of their albums, but that any self-published book is immediately under suspicion as being complete garbage ? The paradox feels like a Magnolia-backed one, though it's more likely one they simply condone. If you happen to be at a party where the subject comes up, mention that Dickens self-published *A Christmas Carol* and that all those Peter Rabbit books were self-published too. Muse aloud about when exactly cultural gatekeepers were suddenly deemed so essential.

Something about me that people, especially my wife, find astounding is that I've known very little of death in my own life. If you don't count my parents, that is, who died in a house explosion when I was seven. I guess you could argue that their deaths were enough trauma for a lifetime, and that the carousel my life became after ensured I would only be passing through people's lives, not staying for the final curtain. Once, when I was in high school, I caught a whiff of the perfume of a girl who waltzed pass me, something like burned cinnamon, and for the rest of the day I thought of the mother I never got to really know, sure that she'd worn a similar scent. But I was only trying to convince myself it was real. Earlier that week our English teacher had asked us to write a personal essay involving something to do with family, and while I thought I'd written a cohesive piece about my foster family, the Chandlers, my prick English teacher, this balding douchebag who had once been some kind of judge, asked me about my birth parents. That's the kind of place my high school was, an all-boys prep school that Mr. Chandler had gotten me into, since it was his alma mater and he was what you would call a legacy. I stammered out a half answer about how I never really knew my birth parents, before slinking away, and I tortured myself for days after about why I couldn't remember one thing about them. My only memory was

of a little girl who'd lived next door. Maybe *she* was the one who'd smelled of burned cinnamon.

Once, when I was ten—this was when I was in Santa Fe with the McCallahans, my first official foster family after my grandparents briefly took me in—I remember waking one day near Christmas to find all the adults in a trance, shoulders stooped in sadness. I thought maybe the president had been shot, based on my learning about the Kennedy assassination earlier that year, but it was explained to me that John Lennon, one of the Beatles, had been murdered in New York City. I hardly knew who the Beatles were, but the effect of John Lennon's death on seemingly everyone everywhere in Santa Fe and beyond made an impression on me. I felt the pain the death was causing people, the anguish in their hearts. And I silently tracked the days and weeks and months before it appeared to lift, if not forever. When I hear about someone dying, I think of the cycle of denial and acceptance that I witnessed firsthand so long ago and understand that, for the loved ones of that someone, the early stages of the cycle are just beginning.

Why, if we can remember little else about someone, do we remember how he or she died? The last moment of a life is mostly irrelevant when applied against how that life was lived. Admit it: when you're watching an actor in a movie who you know has died in a peculiar way, you're thinking about that strange death. You're looking at the actor on the screen and thinking, *You have no idea how you'll die, or when, but I know.* Do we prefer to keep a catalog of endings as possibilities for our own final moments? Our obsession with the beginning, middle, and end lends unearned weight to endings, which are mostly elusive, except for death.

Every year you pass the anniversary of your death without even realizing it.

Our fascination with bizarre and even gruesome deaths is unfortunate, reducing the victim's life to the final act. You're thinking of one as you read this, and even if you can appreciate other facts about the person's life, or admit intellectually to his or

her contributions to society, the paramount fact in your mind is the way that person died.

Know the painting on the cover of the Duran Duran album *Rio* by Patrick Nagel? Up to that point, paintings by Nagel were primarily found in *Playboy*. And before that, like Andy Warhol, he was an illustrator with corporate clients like Budweiser. He also designed Whitney Houston's mom's record album, among some others. Nagel also died young, of a heart attack, not yet forty, after participating in a celebrity aerobathon in Santa Monica, which, ironically, was to raise money for the American Heart Association. The aerobathon lasted fifteen minutes. Nagel made it as far as his car in the parking lot.

A lot of us in Arizona spent what little money we had on posters of Nagel prints at Spencer Gifts. Every mall had a Spencer's, and you could flip through the posters in the back, near the sex toys and other adult-themed merchandise. I once went to a house party that had a signed original Nagel hanging on the wall. Rumor was they were scarce, and I spent most of the party—a high school rager during my public school days at Leone Cooper High, before I transferred to private school—sipping watered-down beer from a red plastic cup and glancing at the original Nagel. Nagel painted beautiful women for *Playboy*; Thomas Kinkade painted cottages that glowed for Christians.

Another '80s icon, the author of the novel *The Hitchhiker's Guide to the Galaxy*, Douglas Adams, also died at forty-nine, and also after working out in California. Copies of the novel were as prevalent as Nagel posters. The zany adventures of Arthur Dent fit snugly into the Dungeons and Dragons culture that had gripped a lot of American youth. Whether or not you were in the know depended on your knowing the answer to the Ultimate Question. (Spoiler alert: it's 42.)

Whose death sucked more: James Dean's or Jayne Mansfield's? Or Orville Redenbacher's, whose involved drowning in a Jacuzzi?

Those "Which Pop Culture Character Are You?" quizzes are

about as accurate as fortune cookies, but absent any religious or political persuasion, both things you generally inherit from your parents, I can easily trace my personality through its pop culture influences. I realized it only recently, when Vanessa was out with her friends for going-away-but-not-really-leaving drinks at her favorite dive bar on the Lower East Side, and I happened across an old episode of the television show *M*A*S*H*. A long-buried memory surfaced, from my stay with the Alexander-Degners in Rapid City, about how much my foster parents loved the show. It always seemed to be on the console in their den, the old TV that weirdly also housed a record player under a wooden flap on top. The show was of no particular interest to me, but catching it again all these years later, I immediately recognized how much my personality aped that of chief surgeon Benjamin Franklin "Hawkeye" Pierce. The similarities were disturbing: the cynical but humorous deflection, the indignation that gives way to rage when finally pushed.

Then I thought: *Maybe I was born with a cynical, indignant personality, and so are a lot of other people, and Hawkeye Pierce is just a stereotype of people like me.*

But what children are born cynical and indignant? The *M*A*S*H* influence feels true, disturbing as it is, since it opens up the real possibility that our throwaway culture is actually having a formative effect on us. Did a child grow up to be a bit of an asswipe because he or she loved Calvin and Hobbes? Or did all those Garfield cartoon strips convince kids that it was okay to be a bully? Do Eminem's fans hear his multi-Grammy-winning music as satire and fantasy created by his alter ego, Slim Shady, or do they just hear anthem? Was John Lennon murdered because of *The Catcher in the Rye*?

Is art responsible for its influence?

Is there a danger in making everything so egocentric?

Or is there no escaping egocentrism? And if so, does that prove second chances are a frivolous nicety more about the forgiver than the forgiven? How hard is it really not to say the thing you're not supposed to say, not to behave the way you're not supposed to? Do

those who transgress reveal their true personality, letting the mask slip, or will they genuinely get it right the second time around? Can a life truly be corrected?

Is it okay to muddle through the long middle of our lives without considering these questions and others?

Is our upcoming move to the Hudson River valley more of the middle, or will it precipitate the end of our story together, or the actual end of one or both of us? As the apartment fills with boxes, the question remains unresolved. Our end could be in an as-yet-undetermined place, one familiar or unfamiliar to us, and our relationship to each other could be as strong or stronger than it is today, or it might be like those colored refractions you find in a kaleidoscope. Related, but without a clear bond. Will any of us be afforded the opportunity to ponder the end? Do we want that?

At least we can take pleasure in knowing our beginning. Not our birth, thankfully, or even the first however many number of years, when we practice living before generating our first memory. And not even our first memory. Our true beginning is that moment everyone can trace back to mark the Before and After in their lives. For me, it was a moment in my teens, late in my high school life, when you could feel the pressure to become something not exactly bearing down, but beating its wings off in the distance. That time was infused with possibilities, and whether true or not, the pool of what you could do was a lot larger and deeper than anything you couldn't. But decisions would have to be made, which would or wouldn't come to bear on the outcome of how your life would turn out, and circumstances would inevitably prevail, which again might or might not dictate how things went. A neighbor had borrowed her parents' car, and the two of us plowed through the desert heat from Phoenix to Los Angeles to visit a friend of hers. I hadn't been back to California since I lived on Sterne Street in San Diego, and I'd forgotten more about Southern California than I remembered. We hit traffic as we entered the city and inched slowly toward her friend's house. Night began to fall. We rolled down the windows as

we neared our destination, the lush greenery surrounding us like a hug as we breathed in the cool marine layer, a mist hovering in the air. You couldn't see the ocean, but you sensed its nearness. Our favorite song came over the radio just as a light up ahead cycled from yellow to red, and we slowed, stopped, and sat silently, listening, breathing, in no hurry for the light to change.

II. We Are All of Us Kidding Ourselves

EVER NOTICE HOW WHEN YOU'RE SINGING ALONG TO YOUR favorite song, the memorized lyrics don't really register, but if you think about them, they don't make a lot of sense? Or if you speak them without the music, they border on nonsense? The Red Hot Chili Peppers immediately come to mind, those Seussian rhymers, and also "Come on Eileen" by Dexys Midnight Runners, the '80s anthem we all lost our minds to when the familiar *bump-da-bump, bump-da-bump* issued forth, never mind the lyrics (not to mention the band's name: What does "Dexys Midnight Runners" even mean?). But really I'm talking about the pop lyrics we sing in the private karaoke of our cars and homes that we'd be hard-pressed to explain if anyone quizzed us. We're talking about space cowboys, bohemian rhapsodies, bags of sunshine, bullets with butterfly wings, drops of Jupiter. R.E.M.'s "Losing My Religion," even though we're *sure* it means something. Same for "Once in a Lifetime" by Talking Heads.

My wife, Vanessa, maintains her collegiate allegiance to the music of Beck, a singer whose song "Loser" certainly qualifies. And even though I'm an avowed Beck nonfan, I'd allow the argument that there might be metaphor within and that being a monkey in the time of chimpanzees could mean something to someone somewhere. I guess the reason I'm even bringing it up is because recently Vanessa and I were driving home from a weekend wedding

in Maine, and a song I remembered everyone loving by a band that isn't Hootie and the Blowfish, but whose music sounds like it was written for Hootie fans, came on, and even though I hadn't heard the song in forever, and even though I actively loathed the song when it was on everyone's lips, I found myself singing along. Vanessa claimed she didn't know the song, but she was obviously lying, a sometimes-charming trait of hers.

Theme songs for movies are a different animal, I suppose, since the artists are hired for the express purpose of writing a song about a movie, or at least incorporating elements of the film into their ditty. Cutting footloose isn't really a thing, except on film, nor is falling in love between the moon and New York City. The writing of those songs is more like homework for the songwriters, and sometimes they luck into a hit pop song, but those songwriters can't be held to account is, I guess, the point.

Which, in your opinion, were better: the films of the 1970s or movies from the 1980s?

Where you land on that question probably depends on your age, since nostalgia weighs more heavily in these kinds of debates than anything that can be asserted as fact. I had an older foster brother when I lived with the Alexander-Degners in Rapid City who would watch movies only from the '70s. In particular, the first two *Godfather* movies, which he would quote unbidden at all times of day. *The Last Picture Show* was another. I'll admit I found that one more interesting than his other favorites, especially the swimming pool scene. But most of the movies my foster brother—fuck was his name?—watched were war movies, or about coming home from the war. *The Deer Hunter* was a big one. And also *Apocalypse Now.* The only movie from that era I really dug was *Chinatown*, but my foster brother didn't share my enthusiasm for it, so I didn't see it again until later in life, when I also saw *One Flew Over the Cuckoo's Nest, A Clockwork Orange, The French Connection, Serpico, Network,* and the Monty Python movies. Oh, and *All the President' s Men.* Love that movie. But seeing them retrospectively is one thing; watching them

as they were released in theaters, like chapters in the story of your life, must've been quite another.

What's curious about the films of the 1980s is that rather than spooling out the story of our lives, there seemed to be a concerted effort to distract viewers with fantasy and adventure, like the Indiana Jones movies, *E.T.*, *Back to the Future*, *Field of Dreams*, *Top Gun*, *Dirty Dancing*, *Bill and Ted's Excellent Adventure*, *Footloose*, *The Lost Boys*, and other fare meant to sell popcorn and little else.

The movies closest in ambition to those of the '70s had to be films like *Brazil*, *Scarface*, *Once Upon a Time in America*, *Tootsie*, and the war movies (again) *Platoon* and *Full Metal Jacket*. But more people had seen *E.T.* and Indiana Jones than had seen these titles. Which is to say that they didn't pop up in everyday conversation, weren't part of the zeitgeist the way the studio movies were.

Less so, even, were the movies my friends and I loved the most: *Heathers*, *Blue Velvet*, *Do the Right Thing*, *Better Off Dead*, *The Princess Bride*, a bootlegged copy of *Withnail and I*, all of which went on to become classics. We loved some of popular films too: *St. Elmo's Fire*, *Beetlejuice*, *Stand by Me*, *The Shining*, the *Vacation* movies, *Dead Poets Society*.

And, of course, the films of John Hughes. The Hughes movies were so aligned with our lives, they felt like documentaries. A symbiosis of experience existed between us in the seats and the characters on the screen. And the music became the soundtrack by which we lived. In the pre-internet days John Hughes was a mysterious figure. The popular line about him then was that he treated teens like they were adults, took their problems seriously. It was like having our own patron saint.

Those "Which John Hughes Character Are You?" quizzes came along much later than the films, and they miss the subtle point that we envisioned ourselves as all of the characters, in some way or another. We were both Ferris and Cameron. We were parts of Andie and Duckie and Blane and, sadly, Steff. The entire Breakfast Club. The love story between Jake and Samantha at the heart of

Sixteen Candles, echoed by Steff's unrequited love for Andie in *Pretty in Pink,* telegraphed that all the social stratospheres we knew might not be real, or at least as real as we'd been led to believe. And the kiss Watts and Keith share in *Some Kind of Wonderful* made us question if we might be in love with our opposite-sex friends, something we'd probably been wondering from the start. The movies have their faults—Long Duk Dong, Anthony Michael Hall's character having sex with an unconscious girl, Bender's bullying Claire until she acquiesces, the casual homophobia throughout—but the racism and homophobia and bullying were a part of our high school experience and so it felt truer than not.

I was living in New York the day John Hughes stumbled in front of a Midtown French brasserie and died of a heart attack. Like that, the storyteller of our youth was gone. The world had moved on, and while his films were still considered teen classics, any discussion of a love for them had to include the disclaimer of all they didn't do in terms of inclusion and diversity, as well as the aforementioned problems. It's important to have an intimate relationship with your shortcomings, and these movies help remind us of who we were, and who we've become, and who we'd like to be.

News of Hughes's death flashed around the world, and when out of curiosity I ambled by the sixteen candles someone had set up as a memorial in front of the bistro, along with a picture of Hughes, I felt less than I'd hoped. I spotted the scaffolding ahead and crossed the street. The first thing I overheard when I came to New York was "Never walk under scaffolding."

You know who isn't afraid of anything? Travel superstar Rick Steves. One thing I'd love to know is how ol' Rick is able to commit to his life in the community where he lives his personal life when his professional life has taken him all over the world and introduced him to all sorts of people, many who may be more interesting than the ones that populate his everyday life. When he's home in the Pacific Northwest, is he daydreaming about that overnight sailing from Stockholm to Estonia he enjoyed in the company of the

friendly local who showed him the best places to eat? When he's in line at Starbucks, is he dreaming about the Turkish coffee brewed in a copper pot, remembering how he had to cut it with a little sugar, which marked him as a tourist? Or is he able to forget the people and the places (and the meals!) the minute he steps on the plane for the next destination? And do the people and the places blur together ever? I'd love to buttonhole him at a party to find out if he just lives in the moment, same as I learned to from moving around so much in my youth. Friday you might be in class sweating next week's exam, rolling your eyes at your friend two rows over at something the teacher said, not knowing that come Monday you'd be in another state, at another school, sizing up your new classmates for allies or identifying instant enemies.

I imagine me and Rick Steves have the same skill set. You immediately accept the new reality and set to work navigating it. Sure, ol' Rick has his family and his business waiting back home, the same smiling faces at the gate when he returns to the airport; but while he's away, he's untethered, and can he really count on a safe return to his previous, comfortable life? Perhaps, but perhaps not.

Maybe Rick agrees with me that that moment in movies when someone begs for his or her life at the hands of a villain is trite and pointless. You can't change your circumstances by begging or bargaining. I hate those phony scenes in movies. I'd like to imagine that if in a similar situation, me and Rick would just look at the villain and think, *This is where we are now, where the hands have come to rest on the clock.*

Same for enduring painful end-of-life treatments. Is it healthy to waste your last energies fighting against an imminent and fast-approaching future? Me and Rick would tell you just to go with the inevitable and resist the understandable urge to conquer what is unconquerable.

A friend of mine who died gracelessly because he tried to conquer the unconquerable was preoccupied at the end of his life

with whether or not saxophones should be employed in the making of pop music. Uncounted hours were spent in his last days arguing over the merits of saxophone in songs like "Careless Whisper" by George Michael, or Bowie's "Modern Love," or even Springsteen's "Born to Run." He admitted digging the sax in Men at Work's "Who Can It Be Now?," arguing that the saxophone was instrumental to the chorus and thus to the title. But he was dubious about Hall and Oates's "Maneater," hated Billy Joel's "Scenes from an Italian Restaurant"—a song he loathed violently for reasons he took to his grave—and even the terrific saxophone solo in Whitney Houston's remake of Dolly Parton's "I Will Always Love You."

Remember when Dolly Parton's name was code for "big tits"? I can still remember my seventh-grade friend making the gesture with his cupped hands, holding them out in front of his chest, and we all nodded wisely. We were in the know. There were tits, and then there was Dolly Parton. Her breasts were an exaggerated cartoon of breasts. Even her name, Dolly, lent itself to parody. We wouldn't know until much later that she was a trailblazer, but think about the *decades* of sniggering she'd have to put up with first. That's a lot to ask of anyone. You couldn't endure that, be honest. You'd give up, or give in, maybe go along with the joke, maybe make the joke yourself before anyone else could bring it up.

Most of us can mark the period in our lives when we received wisdom versus when we started to think for ourselves. Maybe high school or college, or maybe just as our experiences accrued, as we began to live our lives. That moment when we saw how useful shorthand was, how much easier it was to distill something it may or may not be, for our convenience, and for the convenience of communicating the idea to those around us.

Punky Brewster was a character I was vaguely aware of, but I was too old for the show when it was on TV, though I knew immediately when the actor who played Punky grew breasts that were too large for her body. I knew a woman in Florida back in my bartending days who had the same situation. She was okay with the

attention, but she felt like her extraordinarily large breasts were a thing she brought with her, rather than being a part of her, if that makes sense. She'd make jokes about them and acknowledge them for their attributes, but as if admiring an actor in a film. Nothing but complimentary, but also recognizing that they had very little bearing on her as a person. If society valued them over everything else, what could she do? She said it was like seeing a Ferrari on the highway: Who cared who the driver was? I never knew if I was projecting my own sadness onto her situation, if people couldn't see past her double-Ds to the actual person she was, or if she was comfortable in her amusement in people's reaction to her enormous breasts. Or if she simply liked the attention. *No shame in that*, I remember thinking, and also that it might be a kind of superpower.

When I was in the fifth grade, in Santa Fe, the principal called my foster mother to alert her to the fact that I was playing only with girls on the playground at recess. Mrs. McCallahan mentioned it in passing, giving no indication it was a matter for concern; but I was self-conscious thereafter, caught between wanting to gossip with the girls in my class on the swing set and tossing a basketball into the netless hoops on the basketball court with the cluster of boys whose approval or at least acceptance I'd need to survive the days. Someone with a modern sensibility would recoil at the principal's insinuation, but the principal is exonerated by the simple truth that it's unseemly for men to be friends with women they are not married to or interested in as a romantic partner. Vanessa would lose her mind and it would be a source of disquiet if I started going to the movies with her friend Laurel, or if I met her friends Amanda and Donna for coffee during the week. Sure, I could easily ask their husbands, also friends of ours, to the movies or for coffee, but I wouldn't. And if Laurel's or Amanda's or Donna's husbands caught wind of my taking in a movie or having coffee with their wives, they would feel uncomfortable if not hostile at the idea. And, worse, others in our circle would assume that I was either sleeping with these women or that I wanted to. We're not responsible for other

people's assumptions, clearly, but who among us would flout the status quo? Suddenly a film matinee is more of a hassle than giving in to the notion that it isn't okay to be friends with the opposite sex.

The problem, of course, is the superpower women have over men, namely that if they proffer sex, of any kind, it takes a pretty rare type of man to refuse. The woman I knew in Boca Raton knew this. She could harness the power of her oversize breasts at will. It's why the sexually free and liberated woman is a threat to the equilibrium the world knows. A woman walks into a bar and she knows she can have sex with anyone she chooses; whereas the ritual of manhood involves positioning oneself so as to become desirable to the opposite sex, vying to be chosen. Some rely on personality, others on their innate good looks. But if you're a man, you're on a continual quest to be discovered. Conventional wisdom has it that women are the ones caught in a perpetual contest for attention, but if the truth is spoken, it's undeniable that women hold all the power, something that was maybe on the principal's mind when he thought to pick up the phone and dial my foster parents' number to deliver the cautionary warning about my future, based on my predilection for playing with girls on the playground at recess.

Do you think Peter Falk was embarrassed at the commercial success of *Columbo* and frustrated by the lack of the same interest in his film work, much of it avant-garde? All those movies he made with the auteur John Cassavetes? And what in the world would Columbo's audience think if they saw Falk's Archie Black in the film *Husbands,* treat the Japanese girl in the film the way he treats her? Wonder if Falk thought one audience had no idea about his other audience, that he was living an artist's double life. The episode of *Columbo* that features both Falk and Cassavetes is telling, the one where Cassavetes plays a conductor cheating on his wife, played by Blythe Danner. (If you look closely, you can see she's a little bit pregnant with future film star Gwyneth Paltrow.) Many of the tête-à-tête conversations between Falk's Columbo and collision of art and commerce.

The most well-known episode of *Columbo*—the one featuring a team of successful mystery writers, played by Jack Cassidy and Martin Milner, whose partnership is dissolving (and ends with one murdering the other)—was directed by future legend Steven Spielberg. In an early scene Cassidy's character utters the line, "In the mystery writer's soul, it is always the middle of the night." The line establishes the character as the wittier and showier of the two, which becomes part of the plot, and the English majors watching at home might've heard the echoes of F. Scott Fitzgerald's line from his famous work *The Crack-Up*: "In a real dark night of the soul it is always three o'clock in the morning." Hollywood has forever been the final resting place of those with literary ambitions— Fitzgerald famously tried to apply his talents to the film industry, with disastrous results—and not knowing that the *Columbo* quote is based on the Fitzgerald quote is harmless and as innocuous as not realizing a new favorite song is a cover. Knowing the source material certainly doesn't add any extra layer of meaning to the show; it just reveals that the script was written by someone who either had a passing knowledge of literature or was an avid reader of Fitzgerald.

An interesting extrapolation, though, is that obviously nothing comes from nowhere, or rarely. And that sometimes inauguration is no guarantee of posterity (e.g., first-generation Cassavetes's conductor have a meta quality to them, as if the two are aware of the violent technology), and what really counts is *popularization*. Love *Ocean's Eleven* and its sequels? Try watching the original featuring the Rat Pack. As painful as the days of waiting for your phone and modem to connect so you could scour bulletin boards for the latest messages. More people alive today could tell you something about that *Columbo* episode—or *Columbo* in general—than have heard of Fitzgerald or, certainly, have heard of *The Crack-Up*.

Another skill you acquire from being shuttled from place to place is the ability to argue both sides of a thing in order to survive, to never offer an opinion. How to lead conversations without saying anything, but at the same time getting the other person to open up.

When the girl who sits in front of you in Ms. Saltonstall's second-grade class thinks the boy in the front row smells bad, you think he stinks too. And when the boy in the front row who may or may not stink professes his love for baseball, you admit that you love baseball too. You become a human thermometer, but also a bit of a game show host. You want the people around you to feel relaxed and, more importantly, to like you, but to like you in a *general* way. You learn quickly that specificity is poison to your mission and that what you're mostly trying to do is disappear in plain sight. What you care about, the things you like, are not just of no importance, they are to be denied, and of course somewhere along the journey the erasure becomes complete and you can't remember how you feel about anything, or if you care to have a feeling about it.

For a brief moment, in a land and time that seems far removed from my life, I actually argued for this or for that. My fifth-grade teacher in Santa Fe, Ms. Fisher, a recent widower, gave me the extra attention in class that other kids punished you for on the playground and invited me to her Toastmasters club, which met at the local public library once a week. I knew my foster family, the McCallahans, would not rearrange their work schedule to drop me at the library, and I demurred, but Ms. Fisher offered to drive me to and from, which the McCallahans agreed to, if only to have the request go away.

The interior of Ms. Fisher's small car was overpowered by the cherry air freshener hanging from her rearview mirror, the cardboard cutout of two red cherries outlined in yellow and black bouncing as we navigated the short distance from the McCallahans' to the public library downtown. Ms. Fisher cranked her window halfway so that she could smoke, eyeing me as she flicked mentholated ash into the night air.

The fluorescent lighting in the library conference room cast dark shadows across the faces of the other Toastmasters. I didn't realize until the moment I inched my blue plastic chair up to the table that I'd be the only kid. I also didn't realize that many of the

other Toastmasters were teachers at Lewis and Clark Elementary, or that the principal would be at the head of the table, manning the wooden timer that let speakers know when to begin (green light), when they had thirty seconds to finish (yellow), and when they had to stop, even if midsentence (red). I can't recall the topic I was given to argue, but I remember the satisfied air around the table when I successfully engaged the assignment, the others having no idea that I'd been training for Toastmasters my entire life.

At that wedding in Maine that Vanessa and I attended, lighted tents were erected to serve as bathrooms for the attendees. You had to imagine the design for the women's tent was more thoughtful than the circular trough filled with ice in the men's, all of us in suits coloring cubes of ice yellow while trying not to glance across the way to the stranger doing the same or, worse, the guy we'd met with our significant other moments earlier, exchanging pleasantries about nothing. As I trod the thick lawn outside the tent, I overheard two bridesmaids holding each other as they exited their tent, one bridesmaid lamenting the weight gain of another bridesmaid. I crossed their path intentionally, maybe in an effort to shame them, but they motored through, oblivious to my presence, and I was left with the not-startling realization that women are pretty good at policing their own, dictating how they should look or act. Different from men, who go out of their way not to engage with other men and their deficiencies, unless a confidence is sought. As the bridesmaids sauntered toward the dance floor, I thought about all the mothers who likely told their daughters to keep a nice figure with the hopes of meeting a nice businessman, and from there my mind plummeted to the depths and the entire evening was ruined.

Be honest, the music of Metallica is unnecessary, right? How strange is it that a random collection of musicians can come together and their music can be consumed en masse, for a moment, for whatever reason, but hindsight brings the realization that we the audience were only using that band and their music to live our lives at that particular moment in time? Maybe you're violently disagreeing

with that hypothesis, but when your favorite Metallica song next blares, are you transported into the distant past, or is the song relevant to your life now? Is the true function of music to archive? Is your favorite song by your favorite band tinged with nostalgia immediately after it means something to you in the present tense?

And whatever happened to all those cassette tapes where we spent hours waiting for our favorite song to come on the radio, running to press the black play and red record button at exactly the same moment, the satisfying click and the rotating spools on the cassette tape assuring us that we'd captured it perfectly? Of course, the savvy among us would just wait for the *American Top 40* countdown hosted by Casey Kasem. Guessing where your favorite song would land in the hours-long radio show was another matter, not to mention the anxiety induced by the padding of the show with various trivia, recaps, the list of "great radio stations" that carried *AT40* "around the world," and the dreaded Long Distance Dedication.

I was an embarrassingly advanced age before I learned that Kasem was also the voice of the character Shaggy on *Scooby-Doo*. (Different from the confusion about how the actor who played Darth Vader in *Star Wars* was not the actual voice of Darth Vader, a real head-scratcher.) Like a lot of things, once you know it, it seems obvious. If you catch a rerun and hear Shaggy say, "Like, Scoob, let's get something to eat," something deep in your core braces for another Long Distance Dedication. But before you're hip to that piece of trivia, the two pop culture poles seem as distant as Pluto and the sun. What in the hell does a stoner who can understand his Great Dane have to do with Lionel Richie or Huey Lewis and the News or Whitney Houston? Only an abnormal mind would connect those dots, but once they're connected for you, Pluto crashes into the sun.

Vanessa occasionally ribs me about my lack of sartorial splendor, and I told her about an article I'd read that stated unequivocally that not only did geniuses wear black T-shirts, as I did, but that they often

wore the same clothes day after day. She characteristically rolled her eyes at this, and I editorialized that perhaps they weren't geniuses, per se, as the article intimated, but for sure they understood the value of focusing their attention on what mattered, not which colors went with which. That's how average people remained average, I argued. I went a step further and posited that the Powers That Be benefited greatly when you were bogged down in this kind of minutiae, so that you were completely worn down when it came to decisions that mattered. If everyone exasperates all their discernment on the trivial, they'll more easily give in to whatever popular opinion comes their way. Vanessa didn't buy the argument, but I could sense the seed had been planted.

Know what's completely daft? It only occurred to me on the zillionth viewing, and long after Vanessa and I had started taking turns brandishing one of Columbo's signature lines—"I sorta knew it right from the beginning"—but Lieutenant Columbo's cynical suspicion of the *first* suspect he encounters presages my own generation's suspicion about *everything*. The cleverly rumpled lieutenant's massively appealing bumbling, often milked for every last ounce of comedy, wasn't just a disguise meant to disarm the suspect, it was also meant to charm the baby boomer audience into forgetting for a moment that their hard-won distrust of everything and everyone would give rise to a hypercynical generation of offspring who would never trust anyone or anything, no questions asked.

Don't take my word for it; watch any late-night rerun and marvel at how quickly Columbo questions what he hears from someone he knows to be a witness but who is soon also the prime suspect. His doggedness is always rewarded, and while we the audience know from the outset that he's onto the right person, we recognize in ourselves the suspicion that we aren't being told the entire truth and that what we *are* being told, like as not, won't stand up to scrutiny.

Yet the kid who drank Coke while eating Pop Rocks definitely died.

And the government is for sure keeping secret a colony of

extraterrestrials somewhere in the Nevada desert.

Oh, and *Disney on Ice* is an inside joke about how Walt Disney's head is cryogenically frozen and that he plans to rejoin society once science "figures it all out."

When I moved foster homes in the middle of my freshman year, leaving the cold winters of Rapid City and the Alexander-Degners for the sun and sand of San Diego and my new family, the Wallaces, my next-door neighbor, a girl whose name I can't recall, was selling something called Tom-Wat to try to earn enough money for an eighth-grade trip to Disneyland. She knocked on the door, a cardboard suitcase at her tiny feet emblazoned with the company's name. She asked if she could come in and show her wares. I told her the Wallaces were at work and that I didn't have any money, but she grabbed the cardboard suitcase with both hands and lugged it into the Wallaces' foyer, where she popped the lid and spread out the rose-scented candles, a frosted-glass dove light, hand-painted wooden Santa ornaments, a twin-bladed nail clipper, fruit- scented erasers, thermal travel mugs, a universal multiwrench, and a magnet that read "Taste Makes Waist." Nothing seemed to cost more than two dollars, and I idly wondered how in the world she was going to sell enough merchandise for a weekend in Disneyland. I knew the Wallaces kept some spare change in a tin San Diego Padres bucket in the garage, and I mined it for as many quarters as I could find, the girl cupping her hands together to receive the bounty. I told her to keep her stuff, but she handed me a rose-scented candle. I smiled and kept it in the drawer of my nightstand until the acrid smell of artificial roses overpowered my tiny bedroom and I tossed it in the kitchen trash compactor.

A couple of days ago I was humming along in my car when a black Audi turned out of a Starbucks in front of me, necessitating my applying the brakes in a manner that disrupted not just my trajectory, but the entire flow of traffic. I didn't honk, though I admit I swerved dramatically into the empty left lane and then swerved again to take my rightful place ahead of the Audi, as if to highlight

the driver's negligence. But more than that, I burned with the same anger I always do when someone abuses the idea that we should all look out for one another. The everyone-else- will-look-out-for-me attitude is maddening. These drivers know you don't want to wreck your car when you could easily slow down, though you'd love to point out how they could easily wait their turn, rather than darting out into traffic with the assumption that no one will crash into them. I wish I didn't fantasize about renting a car for a day and smacking into these careless drivers just to prove their hypothesis wrong. It would be worth doing if there were a guarantee the lesson would be learned, though let's be honest, selfish drivers are likely just as selfish in all aspects of their daily lives, so perhaps the parochial impulse is a foolish one.

These are the same people who would selfishly feel rejected in the face of a loved one's suicide. "Why did so-and-so abandon me?" Or the classic: "How could so-and-so leave me alone to deal?" Hey, guess what, navel-gazer: it had nothing to do with you. You likely weren't even on the person's mind. The same inconsiderate assholes who jump out into traffic wants someone else's choice of suicide to be about them. The feeling of rejection is a powerful one, and selfish people are weirdly always on the hunt for it, as if it fuels their own behavior.

I just remembered that I left out a sad detail about the girl who was selling Tom-Wat in San Diego. She called the trip to Disneyland a "graduation trip," and I pointed out that she was only in the eighth grade. Much later I learned that many of her contemporaries wouldn't make it through high school, so the graduation from middle school would be the last they'd know.

What's sometimes weird is to be of the age that straddles the invention of the internet. Not just the I-remember-a-time-before-the-web thing that makes Gen Xers sound like douchebags, but the feeling of certainty about this or that but not finding any mention of it on the internet because it happened before search engines began cataloging the world's detritus. I spent a solid hour recently trying

to suss out the name of a midnight movie I caught the summer after I was emancipated and quit high school. I was living in my own apartment for the first time, a furnished place in a former Motel 6 in Tempe, the college town built around Arizona State University. The complex housed mostly students, who were often sweating on the plastic lawn furniture around the old motel pool in the courtyard. I was studying for my GED during the day, but the apartments had no air-conditioning, and so the noise filtered in all through the night, making it impossible to sleep.

One night, craving both cool air and solitude, I rode the aqua-colored beach cruiser bicycle I'd stolen from in front of the Coffee Plantation on Mill Avenue to the Valley Art theater, the pink stucco and neon-lit art house that showed movies no one had ever heard of, with actors you might recognize but couldn't readily name. What I remember about the film: a talking ventriloquist's dummy's soliloquy about the nature of time; a plate of fried eggs being dumped on someone's head; a blind priest who hitches a ride with the protagonists. But the title and the rest of the movie eludes me. I asked Vanessa if she knew the film, but she said it sounded less like a movie than a dream, which was of next to no help. Sometimes I forget that she's younger and that we don't have the same cultural reference points.

On the way home from that wedding we attended in Maine, I was teasing her about not knowing that the actor Mark Wahlberg was once a rapper known as Marky Mark, but was at the same time reflecting about the fact that the wedding ceremony we'd just witnessed was likely to be performed, with slight personalization, again tomorrow and the day after, all through wedding season, each couple remembering the day for the rest of their lives as one of the best days of their lives, oblivious to the reality that the wedding venue—in this case a rustic, open barn situated at the edge of a river-fed lake—made its money selling the same experience over and over to brides and grooms who could afford it, creating an enormous population with common, shared memories who would no doubt

insist on the uniqueness of their experience. Even subtracting the venue, the ritual of the marriage ceremony ensures a sameness that is undeniable. That's not to speak cynically about weddings, but rather to acknowledge that at the outset all married couples are bonded by rigidly exacting ritual, however unique their individual situations grow over time, if they do.

One of life's enduring mysteries is how people can't reliably figure out what to do at a four-way stop. Perhaps because everyday driving is done by rote—stop on red, go on green— rolling up to a four-way stop challenges that autopilotness. But those four stop signs are also quite revealing. The driver who rolls through the stop sign regardless of what order they arrived is the same person who changes lanes suddenly without signaling. Then there's the driver who passes up his or her turn to wave on someone else, the same driver who signals well in advance of any turn and then makes a full stop in the road before executing said turn. A four-way stop brings the selfish and the selfless together in a moment in which both can thrive.

Once, someone removed the stop signs at a four-way stop on the west side of Phoenix, dreaming of a fiery crash, but the farmland was so sparsely traveled that the police foiled the plot before it could generate headlines.

Not so the derailment of the Amtrak Sunset Limited in the western Arizona desert in the mid-1990s when someone or multiple someones removed a couple of dozen rail spikes in a quote-unquote political act in retaliation for the government's siege at Waco, or Wacko, depending on your view of the world. The entire train jumped the tracks, and the dining car and sleeper cars fell down a ravine.

I sometimes associate the Sunset Limited derailment and the disappearance of Robert Fisher in my mind, though in reality almost a decade separates the two events. Fisher's West Phoenix home imploded with his family inside, but it was later revealed that his wife and two children had been murdered first. That coupled with

Fisher's disappearance—and the discovery of his wife's abandoned vehicle in northern Arizona, near the Grand Canyon—made Fisher a person of interest and ultimately landed him on the FBI's Most Wanted list.

The sad facts of the terrible crime—and the myth that sprang up around Fisher and his wilderness survival abilities—are always the headline whenever the story is hauled back in front of the public's increasingly divided attention, oftentimes to commemorate the awful event as the years drag on. What likely gets lost in these anniversaries is the stunning blind spot Fisher's father-in-law had when it came to who had likely murdered his daughter and his grandchildren. The nightly news gleefully broadcast the elderly man imploring his son-in-law to return, as if willing his presence back into their lives, confessing his love for Fisher to the camera. The sympathetic would recognize denial as the stage of grief that likely fueled those sentiments, but Robert Fisher's father-in-law's delusion is all of our delusions. Rare are the moments in life when the dots are so easy to connect, so that we all have to admit that not to see it is not to want to see it.

When the dust settles on the twentieth century, or rather when the story of America is longer than a historical eyeblink, *Playboy* magazine and its founder, Hugh Hefner, will be a curiosity to generations to come. Not a curiosity in that the magazine and the lifestyle pioneered by Hefner will be viewed as quaint, or even staid by whatever future pornography awaits, but Hefner's nudity bounties on popular actresses of the day may still shock citizens of the not-too-distant future. That Hefner would let it be known publicly that he'd pay X dollars for your favorite actress to be the nude centerfold of his magazine was a form of open bribery that would surely cause a politician to shudder. And what should the target of the bribe feel? Flattery? Insult? All of that is less interesting than the actress who was forced to *consider* the bounty. *Where am I in my career?* Too early and it might ruin the actress. "Always leave them wanting more" has to be good career advice for any actor, especially those whose

arc has yet to peak. But the pages of *Playboy* were also filled with actresses who felt their careers needed a boost, and so by Hefner will be viewed as quaint, or even staid by whatever future pornography awaits, but it was a difficult equation. Or at the very least a gamble with the likely projected outcome of all gambles.

Vanessa thinks she's being funny when she asks me if every alternative song that comes on the radio is Duran Duran. The joke isn't as good-natured as it might seem, and if I'm being honest, it's probably borne out of my own joke: "Which is your favorite Beatle? Davy or Micky?" Lame, sure, but it fires people up, and even the passionless among us, the ones who would rather wave you through a four-way stop than assert themselves, raise their backs. But I usually defuse the awkwardness with trivia about how the Beatles were in on the joke and were actually friendly with the Monkees, their cynically created doppelgangers. There's something amusing about Paul and John and Ringo and George splashing around a Hollywood pool with the Monkees, perhaps a cloud of pot smoke hovering over the entire scene. Obviously more satisfying to be the inspiration rather than the commercial attempt to monetize the craze, but still. A healthy sense of irony would be enough to see the Monkees through. Except Peter and Micky and Michael and Davy's frustration at wanting to flourish as real musicians, I guess. There's a certain admirable hubris in wanting both commercial success and creative authenticity, especially after signing on to what was clearly an attempt to capitalize on the Beatles' popularity, but hey, not everyone can be Peter Falk, right?

What I don't admit to Vanessa, ever, is that the musical truth for my generation is that U2 is the church, Depeche Mode is the college, and the Cure is our dream life. Instead, I kid her about not knowing what the name Duran Duran is a reference to, and she always just shrugs, unable to remember the title of the Jane Fonda movie that inspired the name, either by choice or because Jane Fonda is not someone her generation knows a whole hell of a lot about. In fairness, my own generation knows her only as a workout hero and

the wife of Ted Turner, the cable magnate, but because we all lost our mind to the video for Duran Duran's song "The Reflex," we've made it our business to know that the band's name comes from the film *Barbarella*, even if hardly any of us have seen it.

None of us saw the movie *Voodoo Swamp*, though a lot of us living in Arizona traipsed through the mansion of Gordon Hall, the Nautilus health club pioneer, who allegedly bankrolled the B movie. Hall's mansion had been built by a Pennzoil heir, and everyone knew it as the house with the helipad on the roof. But when Hall ran into trouble with the IRS, the home became part of a bankruptcy proceeding, and Arizonans queued up to gawk at the 52,000-square- foot house with the fourteen-person Jacuzzi, the racquetball court, and the exercise room with the bathroom doors featuring life-size portraits of Arnold Schwarzenegger.

I took the tour with my high school friend Jason, who used to honk at girls with their boyfriends and yell, "Fuck her! I did!" The line wasn't original to him—he'd heard it from someone else—but each time we rolled down the street in his pearl-colored Mercedes, he couldn't resist. He couldn't have known, nor could I, what just the honk itself did to the couple on the sidewalk. Was the relationship new and therefore the unwanted attention a bothersome source of anxiety for the aspiring boyfriend? Did it give the courted girlfriend confidence or a better negotiating position with her suitor? Or had the relationship run its course? Did the sonorous honking and the probably garbled salutation confirm for the girlfriend that she could do better, and remind the boyfriend of whatever he'd been taking for granted for too long?

The politics of any situation are hardly ever known or realized in real time, however obvious they might be. Could poor Pete Best have known that his firing from the Beatles would make him the most pitiable figure in music history? Though, is it worse to be fired from a band *before* they become famous or after? What about the original lead singer of the rock band AC/DC, whose name no one can remember? Is history more generous to Dave Evans than,

say, Don Felder, Alec John Such, Steven Adler, or Brian Jones, founding members of the Eagles, Bon Jovi, Guns N' Roses, and, holy Christ, the Rolling Stones? Ozzy Osbourne didn't really sweat it when Ronnie James Dio replaced him in Black Sabbath, but it was still a shock to the system, likely. It's sort of like stealing a base in a tight baseball game versus stealing one in a blowout. In a close game players are expected to steal; but in a laugher it's bad form. Pete Best's firing might be considered stealing a base in the late innings, but Ozzy's dismissal was clearly akin to the latter. The overall point is this: right and wrong aren't black and white, but just situational. Which leaks into our everyday lives and leads us into all sorts of trouble. How much easier would life be if it could be lived according to a checklist? Or at the very least by the coding system computers used at the start: If X, then Y. The law operates that way—which sometimes creates an apoplectic population, wanting rights wronged instead of the staid application of laws resulting in predetermined penalties rather than justice, an amorphous idea the law wants nothing to do with.

But we're left adrift with our personal prejudices, which lead to us to make emotional decisions more times than not.

And, of course, inform our personal politics.

Growing up, I would watch *World News Tonight with Peter Jennings* over the other network anchors to try to keep abreast of the news, or, to be honest, to impress my peers and teachers that I knew what was happening in the world. Jennings seemed to me as smooth as any actor as he delivered his lines, and there was something to his wry personality that made it seem like anyone watching was in on any joke. It was a shock, years and years later, after Jennings had died, to read about a study that found Jennings's reporting leaned to the political right. The study even analyzed his facial expressions! That nerdy academic study aside, I'll wager you couldn't find a quorum of average citizens who could've guessed Jennings's politics. The fact that he was Canadian likely made it even more difficult for American viewers to admit he was taking sides.

What was so disconcerting about this study was not the possibility that in my early days I was, without knowing what it was, a right-leaning citizen. Or that I wasn't savvy enough to pick up on the conservative vibe Jennings was giving off. The bone-chilling realization for me when I read about this study was that my life was politics-free, and that while Toastmasters and, more likely, the game-show-host mentality that all my moving around had created aided in erasing any buried. A hundred political scientists could spend a hundred hours studying my facial expressions as I waxed on and on about whatever and never be able to decipher a bias.

You might think that sort of equanimity a kind of nirvana—who among us, except perhaps the hopelessly biased, wish we could suppress our emotional reactions?—but the epiphany was unnerving, and as much as I wanted to discuss it with Vanessa, who would've talked me through it sensibly and maybe pointed out that I'd indicted myself too harshly, I didn't want even a sliver of the notion floating between us.

Also, and maybe a factor more than I cared to admit, I'd had a little smidgeon of a panic attack when our child, Emma, was born, relating to trash collection. I was wheeling our blue and green containers to the curb the night before our collection day when I had the crushing and paralyzing thought that there couldn't possibly be a human-designed system that could contain the amount of trash every person in the world was creating on a daily basis. *Where could all this trash possibly go?* And I suspected that separating our plastic and cardboard from the rest of the trash was just another system we'd invented to give the illusion of control, that it was all gonna opinions I might have about this issue or that, those opinions—my true opinions—were long work out. The spiral from there unspooled quickly as I steadied myself on the curb: I thought about how at one point there had been more land than people, but how that was no longer the case. I thought about how ten dollars was worth ten dollars only because we all agreed it was worth ten dollars, and what if tomorrow we all didn't agree? I gripped the handles of the green

recycling container, rocking it into place the way all my neighbors did, spacing it just so from the blue garbage container, creating the requisite distance the automatic arms on the trucks would need in the morning to execute the chore. Once the containers were lifted into the sky and emptied, and once the trucks thundered a short ways down the block, the trash and recycling were out of our lives forever. Like it had never happened. But the hiss of the trucks' air brakes at the house down the street, and the next, and the next, was an unwelcome reminder that it hadn't gone far, that it hadn't disappeared, as much as you needed it to. The trash collection system was not a real solution, only a fermata, and by the time the garage door slowly lowered, curtaining off the dark night, I could feel my pulse in my temples. I steadied myself before reentering the air-conditioned kitchen, where Vanessa and Emma were engaged in some hilarity. I washed my hands in the sink. A familiar song came over the portable radio next to the stove, and Vanessa began singing it dramatically to Emma, who smiled and smiled and smiled. The song was always on the radio that year, it seemed, and Emma began clapping when I joined in, the joyous moment enveloping us as Vanessa and I belted out the meaningless lyrics with all our hearts, just as we were meant to do, and like we did every time we heard the song for the rest of our lives.

Charlie Martens is the protagonist of the novels *Vernon Downs*, *World Gone Water*, and *Garden Lakes* by Jaime Clarke.